Each One a Miracle

Each One a Miracle

Edited by DeAnna and Terry Ball

Grandin Book Company • Orem, Utah

Grandin Book Company
1170 North Industrial Park Drive, Orem, Utah 84057

ISBN 0-910523-41-X

DEDICATION

Every child deserves a loving family, a home, and a future. Tragically, however, Romania's orphans are kept behind doors which are meant to lock out most adoptive parents and, in some cases, even relief workers. To this day thousands of abandoned children remain in cold, dark orphanages and asylums where often their only escape is death. To those children, this book is dedicated with hope that hearts may soften and doors may once again open.

DeAnna Ball

CONTENTS

INTRODUCTION

NOBODY'S CHILDREN

On Christmas Day 1989, the execution of dictator Nicolae Ceaucescu and his wife Elena brought new hope to the people of Romania. For forty years they had been locked behind the iron wall of totalitarian communism.

Expatriate Romanians returning to their homeland soon learned about thousands of children suffering in state-run orphanages in nearly every town. Through their accounts, the western world came face to face with the grim reality of conditions inside the Romanian orphanages.

Ceaucescu, a power-hungry and cold-hearted dictator, had systematically robbed the population of life-supporting resources, selling crops and other goods on international markets and taking much of the proceeds for his own personal wealth. Then, consumed with the idea of increasing the population of his previously prosperous nation, he abandoned all common sense. He placed heavy taxes upon all couples, even the barren, who did not "produce" at least five children for the state of Romania. Birth control measures were outlawed, and women were checked monthly by Ceaucescu's "Birth Squad" to be certain that their pregnancies were carried full-term. Factory "doctors" were penalized if their factory did not meet monthly birth quotas set by the state. Says one factory worker, "We did not want this, but if you did not submit, you would not be paid your salary. It was so humiliating and degrading, you forgot that you were a person. The conditions in which we were examined were so squalid that we got infections. But there was nothing we could do"(J. M. Paxman, "The Joys Of Motherhood," *Network*, January 1992, 17-29).

Wages were so low and food so scarce that parents could not provide basic necessities for their families. Many children did not survive their first days of life. Ceaucescu responded to this crisis by refusing to issue birth certificates until babies were three months old. Until he issued five birth certificates, couples were forced to pay the heavy tax.

Malnourished mothers had little or no milk for their babies and turned them over to orphanages and hospitals, hoping their children could survive. Healthy children raised by these orphanages were sent to serve in the armed forces or secret police of Romania.

Unfortunately, the orphanages were not equipped to care for the large number of abandoned children they were receiving. Many children became severely handicapped because of the substandard and inhumane conditions. A ratio of one worker to forty babies was not uncommon. In some institutions the mortality rate was as high as 30 percent. Moreover, workers were not well-trained in child care. Babies were tightly swaddled, some for up to two years, causing their arm and leg muscles to atrophy from lack of movement. The only attention most babies received was a daily bottle or two propped into their mouths and an occasional change of swaddling. Their skin blistered from urine saturation, and many babies' eyes became crossed from having nothing on which to focus. Baths were infrequent, and ice-cold water was often all that was available.

On 27 April 1990, Tom Jarriel of ABC's *20/20* showed the world the heart-wrenching scenes of Romanian orphanages. Rooms filled with silent babies rocking themselves for comfort haunted those who saw them. Some orphanage workers appeared to be sympathetic but overworked. "There are only a few of us and so many babies," one worker said.

Several months later on 5 October, *20/20* aired a second program which showed asylums where orphans who were considered imperfect were literally warehoused and given only minimal care. One scene was unforgettably horrible. Naked children, heads shaved, most with visible handicaps from years of neglect, were crowded in unsanitary, unheated rooms, like animals in a huge cage. They sat on a cold cement floor as a worker spooned a few bites of watery soup into their open mouths. Only yards away a second group of children squatted to defecate. One man who was helping to film the scene was overcome with the smell and horror of the situation. "These are human beings!" he moaned. His words sounded a truth that the Romanian communist system had forgotten.

Many of the children had never been allowed to see daylight. Active children were given adult doses of sedatives to keep them quiet, a treatment that often resulted in mental retardation. As many as six children huddled together on a small, blanketless bed for warmth. Some children were found with their hands tethered together with ropes. Many were terrified of their caregivers.

Those thought to be near death were housed in basement rooms where they would not trouble the workers. An American pediatrician found a four-year old boy who was dying from simple anemia; he had never been diagnosed nor given treatment. She found another boy whose ear infection had gone untreated for so long that the outer ear was red and swollen to the size of a baseball.

Those who viewed the segments could not forget them. The *20/20* studio received a greater response from the Romanian series than any other broadcast in its history. Some people, touched by the plight of the handicapped children and knowing that many of their problems could be treated in the United States, traveled to Romania not only to adopt them, but literally to save their lives.

These early adoptive parents blazed remarkable trails that were soon followed by hundreds, and then thousands of others. In early 1991, Sally Jessy Raphael interviewed, Jennifer Lynch, a woman who was so affected by the forlorn look on the face of a three-year-old boy she saw in a news documentary that she traveled to Romania to search specifically for him. After four months of exhausting every lead she could find, she had spent all her money and was weak from lack of food. Because Ceaucescu had only permitted a few phone lines to other nations, Jennifer could not reach her husband in the United States. Just as she was about to leave, she once again dreamed the vivid and disturbing scene that had kept her going for so long. She saw the little boy at the end of a sidewalk, behind a picket fence. In her dream she could see dogs and smell other animals. In desperation, she went to a local police department and described the scene. Touched by her story, someone at the department thought they knew where such a place was located and took her there. It was just as she had seen in her dream: a picket fence, the smell of animals, and a frail little boy with the face she had repeatedly dreamed of at the end of the sidewalk outside the orphanage. Jennifer rushed to him and immediately began the adoption process. Doctors told her that he was so malnourished, weak, and anemic he would have lived only a few days longer had she not come to rescue him.

Each succeeding month brought higher numbers of foreigners adopting Romanian children. At first, each adoption decree had to be signed by the new president of Romania; but later, authority was granted to each county court to grant adoptions within its jurisdiction. This made many more adoptions possible. During 1991, more than eight thousand Romanian children were adopted by people all over the world.

As the adoptions became more numerous, child care workers in Romania began to fear if there were not enough children left in the orphanages, they would lose their jobs and not be able to support their own families. On 1 March 1991, new Romanian laws made entrance to the orphanages by foreigners nearly impossible. No one was allowed to enter without the express consent of a three-person commission headquartered in Bucharest, who would give prospective parents the names of only two children to consider adopting. This policy significantly reduced the number of children from the orphanages that could be adopted.

By June 1991, additional laws were passed which suspended all foreign adoptions of Romanian children. Yet, tragically, additional children were abandoned at the orphanages during the winter of 1991. A reliable count is not available, but individuals returning from Romania report that the orphanages are full. Tens of thousands of babies, children, and youth remain institutionalized. Those children who were adopted during this brief time were the lucky few.

Leila and Mirica Wilson

Lilies of the Field

by Julie Wilson

The words from a blessing I had received echoed in my heart and mind: "Julie, you will face danger in bringing forth your children from Romania, but I bless you that you will be able to boldly step forth and claim them. You will feel the Lord's presence and communicate with him in ways you never have before." If I had known then, not only of the adventure I would experience, but also of the accompanying anxiety and gripping fear, would I have gone ahead? Would I have felt I had the strength to do the things I had to do to bring my children home? In that room, on that day, surrounded by familiar people, places and things, the experiences I would soon face were inconceivable.

I had sought this blessing to aid me on a journey set in motion a year earlier. In April 1990, while leading a perfectly predictable life, I, along with thousands of others, watched in horror and shock as the plight of the Romanian orphans unfolded on the television program *20/20.* Sleep eluded me for many nights. My mind kept rerunning the stark images of those suffering children, those mistreated and wilting lilies from God's field.

Perhaps one reason this program affected me was that we had already adopted two boys, each from birth, who were then two and four years old. A thought kept repeating in my head, "What if my Justin and Garrett were over there, and I didn't go and get them?" That idea was unacceptable to me, so my husband Michael and I discussed the possibility of bringing home one or two of these less fortunate children.

But we were just ordinary people living ordinary lives. How would we go about adopting these children? Where would we start? Because the answers to these questions weren't obvious, and because everyday life once again took over, the issue was pushed to the back of my mind.

Then some months later *20/20* aired another program on Romanian orphans. This time it showed what happened to orphans considered imperfect. The children's imperfections ranged from severe mental and physical disabilities to crossed eyes or large ears. To be honest, I couldn't watch the whole program because the images were too terrible. I did catch the scene that showed four children standing in a corroded tub with water the color of black ink being poured over their bodies as they screamed. And I saw the part where a little girl of about eight years old was descending a worn staircase on all fours because she couldn't stand upright. I saw the scene in which many naked, screaming children were jammed into a small room where they could turn neither right nor left. The atrocities these children experienced were horrors that my heart and mind couldn't and didn't want to accept. That seed planted in my heart in April sprouted and bloomed, but once again I didn't know how to harvest it. But the Lord knew how, for in February 1991 we met a woman who was going to Romania to adopt a child, and she gave us all the information we needed to proceed. The Lord hadn't just opened a window of possibility; he had thrown wide the door. My brother, sister-in-law, Michael, and I were going to Romania for children.

Total reliance on the Lord was necessary from this point on. I had profound promptings that urgency was vital. I felt the door the Lord had opened was closing very quickly, and if we hurried we might just squeeze through its diminishing crack.

Of course once you decide to adopt a child, you can't just get on a plane and head for Romania. The United States Immigration and Naturalization Services (INS) must process a stack of paperwork some six inches high. The process required an FBI fingerprint clearance and a home study, both of which we were told took a minimum of eight weeks.

The eight week delay was a problem because we felt a distinct urgency to leave for Romania as soon as possible and had set a target date of 17 April, just six weeks away. Everyone told us it couldn't be done, but all things are possible in the Lord. Suffice it to say that we had numerous interventions from the Lord on our behalf so that the paperwork was all completed in not eight weeks, or even six weeks, but a mere four weeks.

There was a higher purpose than just our convenience to completing the paperwork quickly. On 31 March we received information that on 1 May the adoption laws would change. We heard speculation that the adoptions would be stopped, and that those already in progress would have to be completed by that date. Because we had come so far so fast, we decided that even with this chilling news we could not quit. We planned to leave on 5 April, just four days away. I rushed around like a wind-up toy wound too tightly, gathering all our food, baby and medical supplies, and every conceivable "must have" item. The real feat was packing this five- to six-week supply into four suitcases. I don't know if it was ingenuity or desperation that accomplished it, but everything was ready for us to leave on 4 April. Then, just as I locked shut my last suitcase, we received a call saying that our Romanian agent could no longer take us as clients. We had no leads for other help.

At this point I sought the priesthood blessing and received those foretelling words. Even though we had no Romanian agent, I knew that the Lord would lead us one step at a time. I knew I was not clever nor sophisticated enough to foresee all the obstacles ahead, but I also knew that there was a power higher than mine at work. After the blessing, peace and a newfound conviction settled upon me.

The next morning, with the sun shining on us, Michael and I boarded our plane, with plans for adventure and high hopes of bringing home our treasure. When we met my sister-in-law in New York, we learned that she had contacted a man in Romania who said he would help us. He had agreed to meet us some 20 hours later outside the Bucharest Airport, holding a card with his name on it. The Lord had helped us take one more step.

The shock of Romania hit me even before the airplane came to a stop. We taxied down a runway full of huge potholes and cracks. Littered on both sides of the tarmac were old and new rusted-out, nonfunctional planes. As the plane came to a halt, soldiers dressed in full combat fatigues, carrying automatic weapons wheeled a rickety set of stairs up to the door. An army tank drove up and pointed its cannon barrel straight at us. I struggled to keep my mounting fright and terror under control. We were escorted to a dilapidated bus that had no seats. Just two old tires lay on the floor in the back to sit on. We chose to stand and hung on to anything we could find, including each other, to remain standing upright.

Once inside the airport, I felt engulfed by a heavy gray cloud. The soldiers were dressed in gray uniforms, the workers in gray lab coats, the people in dated gray apparel. And above this pervasive gray attire was something even more startling, gray faces. The faces still haunt me today, faces with no answering smile, no nods of the head in passing, and most of all, no hope in their eyes. It was like viewing the death of souls.

As we passed through the many check points, I kept looking for a man holding a card. My anxiety grew when he didn't appear. Where would we go and what would we do alone in this totally foreign world? At last we were led through some large double doors which led outside the airport. There we were hailed by some 100 men leaning towards us from a barricade railing. Most of them must have been taxi drivers because I could tell from their gestures that they all wanted us to come with them. We kept walking until at last we saw the man we were hoping would be there to meet us. To me he looked like a long-haired version of Gilligan from *Gilligan's Island.*

We loaded our bags into three extremely small cars and left for the apartment that he had arranged for us. Along the way we saw forlorn, unfinished buildings, some with construction equipment frozen in rust beside them. The city, once known as "Little Paris," was now a cast-off orphan itself. Military soldiers and policemen carried automatic weapons on the streets.

Thirty minutes later we arrived at our apartment. It had no running hot water, no washer or dryer, and no modern appliances, but for me it was a place of safety and security. Each day for the next couple of weeks, I had to force myself to leave this safe womb.

After a day of rest and recuperation, we began our search for adoptable children. Because 3,000 Americans and twice as many Europeans were in Romania looking for children, we decided to begin our search in a little town about two hours west of Bucharest. We were on the road by 7:00 a.m., wedged into a tiny car with no heat and no defroster. We rode with the windows cracked and the cold wind and rain in our faces.

While traveling on the Romanian roadways, I received my second cultural shock as we passed through the peasant villages. It was like stepping back in time one hundred years. The houses were made of adobe brick, some brightly painted, others displaying just a hint of original color. I didn't know it then, but soon I would go into some of those humble homes to adopt my children.

After being on an ill-paved curving road for two hours, we finally arrived in Calarasi. I thought the people living in Bucharest lived hard lives, but I was about to see an even harsher lifestyle. To enter this little town, we literally drove through the yard of a huge steel mill belching red smoke from its stacks. The town was always surrounded either by this red cloud or by the dust kicked up from unpaved roads. On the days it rained—which it did practically every day we were there—the roads became one giant mud hole. We drove through huge puddles, or small lakes, to visit our first orphanage.

Our driver and interpreter went in and asked if we could come in. My heart was practically beating out of my chest as we entered that orphanage. We were not allowed in the area where the children were kept, but were instead led into a small office with a sagging, worn-out couch and an old desk. The staff told us they had two children available for adoption. A nurse brought in a little twelve-month-old boy named Lorenzo. He was beautiful with brown curly hair, big brown eyes, and lashes that any woman would die for. But I noticed that Lorenzo had a blank look in his eyes, the same blank stare I had seen in the eyes of the children on *20/20*. The nurse propped Lorenzo up on the old couch because he couldn't sit up by himself. I picked him up and began to talk and play with him. Michael did the same.

Lorenzo quickly stole a piece of my heart, but deep inside I was hoping to find a girl to take home. With reluctance I went to give him back to the nurse. However, Lorenzo didn't want to go back to the nurse; he wanted to stay with me. When he was finally in the nurse's arms, he turned and, with eyes that were no longer dead, reached out his arms to me. Lorenzo stole my heart completely with his one final act of love.

Michael and I discussed Lorenzo over the next several days as we continued searching for a girl. I felt I couldn't leave Lorenzo in that place to fade into oblivion. Two days later we returned to his orphanage and told the administration that we wanted to adopt Lorenzo. How right it all felt.

Romanian law requires the signature of both the birth

Romanian law requires the signature of both the birth mother and the birth father, if he is listed on the birth certificate, to qualify a child for adoption. The staff at the orphanage told us that Lorenzo's birth mother hadn't been seen for some time, but they gave us her name and the name of her village. Our driver took us to her tiny village. He went into the mayor's office and inquired after the birth mother, but the mayor didn't know her whereabouts. As we were driving back through the village, Michael noticed the one and only tiny store in the village. He asked our driver to go into the store and ask about the mother, because if we could find any news of her, surely we would find it here. He came back in several minutes and said that no one there knew where she was, but perhaps the *Bulibasha* knew. Would we like to meet with him? When we asked him who and what a *Bulibasha* was, he said the *Bulibasha* was the king of the gypsies in that area, and if anyone would know the birth mother's whereabouts, it would be him. Since we had nothing to lose, we agreed.

He went back into the village, led by three or four boys, while we waited in the car. I imagined the gypsies I had seen in movies—the women wearing bright satin skirts and blouses, gold bangles on their ears, arms, and hands, the men wearing brilliantly colored scarves over their heads, gold gleaming from their teeth. With these images in my mind, I didn't know what to expect. In a few minutes my questions were answered.

Coming down the road leading the way was the *Bulibasha*, the king of the gypsies, followed by an entourage of ten to fifteen attendants. He was short and stocky, dressed all in black. What he lacked in stature he made up for in presence. He dealt only with Michael and reported that neither he nor his attendants had heard of Lorenzo's birth mother. With heavy hearts we knew then that we would have to go on and leave Lorenzo behind. I still think of Lorenzo and another little boy named Danny who remain in Romania because we couldn't get them out. I pray often that the Lord has enfolded them in his loving care and protection.

So began the pattern of our lives for the next weeks. Our continuing search took us into many different eye-opening situations. In one village we went into the local doctor's office, an old peasant home with an antique examining table, an antique desk and a glass medicine cabinet. We had to wait there some time, and to occupy myself I began to notice details. I saw in the glass cabinet two petri dishes, one labeled *aspirina*, which I assumed was aspirin. When I walked over to take a closer look, I saw that the dish had only six tablets in it. The dish next to it had about the same number of unidentifiable tablets. In the cabinet was one little Band-Aid, the kind I use on my children, and ten ampules filled with a cloudy serum that I didn't want to identify. Then it hit me that I had carried more medications and prescriptions with me to Bucharest than this doctor had for her whole village. The only thing I saw the physician dispense in the two hours I was there was baby formula, which a doctor must prescribe.

As we left her office, images of my new Romanian friends telling me about their lives came before my eyes. They waited five years for a color television, seven years for a car. It took a quarter of their weekly salary to buy two pounds of meat. One friend asked me about the wonders of a microwave oven, and I told her it took only five minutes to bake a potato. I was humbled when she replied that she stood in line for five hours to purchase a potato. Such inequality is still hard for me to accept. I stood in their bread lines, searched their stores for toilet paper and light bulbs, and hungered with them for a fresh vegetable or fruit that couldn't be found.

Time now either moved in slow motion or whizzed by at warp speed. After two weeks in Romania, my brother and his wife had found their two children, a curly brown haired three-year-old girl with my brother's dimples and my sister-in-law's nose, and a brand-new red-headed infant boy with dreamy blue eyes. Unfortunately, Michael and I had not found our children, and he needed to return to the States. We discussed whether I should return with him, but I felt I had come too far against almost insurmountable odds to quit now. Together we decided that I would continue to search for our children at least one more week.

Michael flew out on a Saturday, a very bleak day for me. The next day, Sunday, I finally found the LDS church. We met in the top of a worn-out building at a school of engineering. The place may have been old and used, but the people inside were bright, new, and welcoming. I had found my oasis in the bleakness of Bucharest. It was my place of strength, of renewal. It helped to carry me through with the difficult decisions and frightening situations I faced on a daily basis.

Monday I went with my interpreter back into the orphanages, the ghettos, the villages, and the hospitals. I found myself walking into four-story ghetto buildings, ascending littered stairways lined with broken windows and marked with neglect and time. I entered tiny two-room apartments where often the only furniture was a bed in the corner. One apartment had soot on the walls because the family had no stove and had to cook over an old oil lamp. Upon leaving these humble apartments, I would often be surrounded by the people from the building, all wanting to touch and talk to me.

I also visited impoverished peasant homes—homes with packed dirt floors, no electricity, and no running water—and looked into prematurely old and weathered faces. One family in a one-room home had no firewood to keep them warm.

Many times I just wanted to run away from it all. But the words from my blessing would return to my mind and give me courage I didn't know I had until just the moment that I needed it—courage to "boldly step forward and claim my children" wherever they might be.

My first week alone passed with my saying a painful goodbye to a seven-month-old little girl named Mariona. I was now into the middle of my second week on my own with no prospect of adopting a child. Time was my enemy. Once again we drove up to a hospital. This time I was asked if I would be interested in seeing a fifteen-month-old little girl. My quick reply was "yes."

In the hospital I actually saw how the children were cared for. I walked down dimly lit halls, some as black as night because there were no light bulbs. The cold radiated up from the flagstone floors, and the walls with their peeling paint gave no warmth. All the workers wore heavy wool coats, styled like gentlemen's bathrobes.

I was led into the children's ward, which consisted of a long hallway with little cubicle rooms off to each side. In these cubicles stood four pre-World War II iron cribs. The babies were clothed in pajamas, which were no more than rags wrapped around their waists. The paint-chipped cribs had stained mattresses with round depressions in the center. The babies' bottoms fit into the depressions, and the mattresses were soaked because the hospital had no diapers. The smells overwhelmed me.

When I saw Leila for the first time, hope and joy filled my soul. My immediate response was, "Yes, I want her." How tiny and beautiful she was! I didn't hold her because she was very shy, but her eyes welcomed me. I didn't need physical contact to know that we were connected on a spiritual and emotional level. With a heavenly disregard for the passage of time, I stayed with her. After I left, her presence lingered with me.

I started the paperwork and prayed hourly that everything would proceed smoothly, for my time had run out to adopt a child, and I couldn't start over. I went every day to the hospital to visit Leila but I always had to search the children's ward for her because they moved her from one cubicle to another.

Before I left for Romania I had felt I would bring home two children, but time had run out for me, and adopting two children now seemed impossible. However, the Lord had higher strategies at work. Six days before Leila's adoption became final, I found her once again in a different hospital cubicle. In the crib next to hers was a tiny baby fully wrapped in hospital pajamas with three hats on. All I could see was its little nose, mouth, and closed eyes. I didn't know if it was a boy or a girl. I inquired after the baby and was told that he was a three-month-old little boy who was available for adoption. In fact, the American couple who was going to adopt him had changed their minds. She had just found out she was pregnant and, being very ill, had left that same morning to return to the United States. My mouth opened and I asked if I couldn't step into their place and adopt this little boy, who was named Mirica. To my delight, all the involved parties agreed. Because the paperwork had already been started, time was once again on my side. It now appeared I would have my two children.

My remaining days were filled with the anguish of waiting while I continually prayed that all would proceed well until the final adoptions, both scheduled on 10 May. The happy day finally arrived, and with great anticipation and tightly strung nerves I arrived in Calarasi. I was to meet my agent at the small, deteriorating courthouse where he was designated to represent me before the judge. I waited and waited outside in the small, cramped car for hours, but he didn't arrive. The court closed at 5:00 p.m. and by 4:30 p.m. I was beside myself with anxiety. Finally, my driver went into the courthouse to see if something couldn't be worked out. While he was gone, the stress of all I had been through erupted, and I began to cry. I prayed for the Lord to take over. I was too emotionally beaten and physically drained to fight any longer. Perhaps it is at times like these, when we have done all that is humanly possible, that the Lord is free to do his finest work. When my driver returned to the car at 4:50 he reported that he had been given permission to represent me in court. I flew out of the car and raced into the courtroom. The proceeding for Leila was over in five minutes, but Mirica's adoption was rescheduled for Friday, two days away.

I went straight to the hospital to pick up Leila. I lifted her tiny little body and held her for the first time. She clung tightly to me. From that moment, she wouldn't let me out of her sight.

We reached our Bucharest apartment about 7:30 p.m., and I couldn't wait to get Leila out of her hospital rags. As I took off layer after layer of old stained clothes, my heart began to pound harder and harder. When she was finally fully unclothed what I saw made my heart ache and my eyes weep. Can there be more wretched sight than a child's body which has been unloved and uncared for? Leila's body was just a skeleton with skin draped over it.

She was sixteen months old and weighed only 12 pounds, the weight of a healthy two or three-month-old baby. Her arms and legs were the diameter of a tube of lipstick. Her stomach was bloated and distended. She was so weak that she could barely sit up. But the most disconcerting thing was her chest. Her rib cage was small and narrow; the only thing that gave definition to her sides were her shoulder blades.

With shaking hands I redressed her in the newborn infant clothes I had brought with me. At 9:00 p.m. that night I took her across Bucharest to the apartment of Dr. Fife, a retired pediatrician who was serving a humanitarian mission for The Church of Jesus Christ of Latter-day Saints. Dr. Fife's only piece of equipment was his stethoscope. He didn't know if her rib cage malformation was caused from a birth defect, a disease since birth, or malnutrition. He listened to her heart and lungs and said all seemed fine there, but he couldn't tell if her small rib cage might be pushing on them. Leila kept her legs tucked up under her and wouldn't bring them down. When we finally got them extended they were so weak they couldn't hold her. Her pitiful arms gave way in the same manner when we placed her in the crawling position. Dr. Fife said he had seen love and good food bring forth miracles in these children. That was the best hope he could offer me at the time. We had access to no modern medical facilities, but we had a better option. I asked Dr. Fife to give Leila a blessing. He blessed her that she would grow strong and normal and have no lasting effects from her shaky beginning in life.

Tears running down my face, I returned to my apartment and tried to get Leila to eat or to drink, but she refused to ingest anything. I placed her on my shoulder and we lay down on the bed together. We slept the whole night that way, Leila never moving a muscle.

The next morning I took her into our tiny kitchen for breakfast, but she still refused to eat. With my hands on her head and a desperate mother's prayer on my lips, I asked the Lord to help her eat. I asked him to show me the way to help her. After I said amen, I listened for a moment, and the words came into my mind to go and get the peanut butter I had brought with me. I took the peanut butter on my finger and placed it on the roof of Leila's mouth, where she couldn't spit it out. After several seconds she began to taste it; she began to like it; and she began to eat.

When Michael called that day I told him what had happened at the court and about Leila's condition. I asked him if we should go ahead with Mirica's adoption, because we didn't know how much medical and individual attention Leila would need. I also told him how the political climate had changed toward adoptions. Ten days after we arrived in Romania, a program was aired on American television that reported baby selling in Romania. After this the tide seemed to change, and visas for the adopted children to return to

America with their new parents were being denied in greater quantities. Visa requests that had passed just weeks before were now being denied.

I had seen several people in distressing situations because their visas had been denied. Their only hope was to apply for humanitarian paroles for their children, a process that was taking another two to three months of waiting. If the humanitarian paroles were denied they had only two choices: they could reabandon their children to a Romanian orphanage, or they could live outside of the United States for two years with their children, after which they could once again apply for a visa. Neither choice was acceptable to me.

Michael and I discussed whether we could get two children out, given these risks. I might be able to get Leila out as a medical emergency, but I was unsure about Mirica. Would he be the stumbling block to our escape? But no child who is loved is ever a stumbling block to its parents, only a stepping stone to greater love. Because we already loved Mirica, we decided to proceed with both adoptions and hope we would all get home somehow.

It was a time of desperate acts by desperate people. Many adoptive parents were losing their jobs or their homes, or going bankrupt while waiting to return home. I knew of several people who had somehow managed to leave Romania and fly into Mexico and Canada. From there they drove across the border with their children into the United States. Two of my friends made it to Yugoslavia but were turned back and forced to return to Bucharest. I knew of a secret 747 airlift that was to take place in the dead of night. We couldn't discuss it with each other over the phone or alert our families at home that we were considering it, because we believed many of our phones lines were tapped.

The daily rumors, coupled with actual events at the American Embassy, rose until the tension was at boiling point.

One distraught American mother thrust her baby into the reluctant arms of an embassy worker and told him to take it. She had been there ten weeks with no help in sight, and she couldn't take it any longer. There were protest marches at the U.S. Embassy with men and women carrying their children in the rain.

This was my darkest time. I felt alone as I had never felt before. I had no country to turn to if I ran into trouble. I felt like a prisoner with little chance of parole, and I hadn't even committed a crime. It was during this time of darkness that the scriptures illuminated my life. On a particularly depressing day, I opened my scriptures at random, and my eyes fell upon this passage from the Book of Mormon:

> *And I will also ease the burdens which are put upon your shoulders, that even you cannot feel them upon your backs, even while you are in bondage. . . . Yea, the Lord did strengthen them that they could bear up their burdens with ease, and they did submit cheerfully and with patience to all the will of the Lord. And it came to pass that so great was their faith and their patience that the voice of the Lord came unto them again, saying: Be of good comfort, for on the morrow I will deliver you out of bondage.* (Mosiah 24:14–16)

I prayed I had enough faith to be delivered on the morrow, whatever morrow that might be.

On 27 May, while I was at the embassy turning in more papers, my husband's name was called out. When I got to the window, I was told that I had been denied visas for both my children. I somehow made it back to my apartment without shedding a tear, but once I closed the door I couldn't seem to stop the flow. When Michael called I could barely make myself understandable, but he calmed and comforted me, telling me that he would move heaven and earth to get us out as quickly as possible. Most of the grief I felt at that time wasn't for me or even Leila and Mirica, it was for my two little boys at home, whom I hadn't seen for more than eight weeks. How much longer must they remain motherless?

The next day, Thursday, I took pictures of Leila into the embassy and described Leila's serious medical condition to a worker. She had me fill out forms to apply for a humanitarian parole, but could promise me nothing. Even so, her "nothing" was better than what I'd had an hour before.

On Sunday afternoon the telephone at the apartment rang. It was an embassy worker calling to tell me that my humanitarian parole had been granted—I could come in the next day and pick it up. I was so excited that I forgot to ask if the parole was for both my children or just Leila. I spent another sleepless night.

The next morning with quaking legs and a shaking voice I asked the all-important question at the embassy window: "Is the humanitarian parole for both my children?" The answer was "yes." How great was my joy, but it was tempered by much sadness as well. I would be leaving behind my sister-in-law with her two children, as well as several other brave, courageous women who will always be my friends—ordinary women who did extraordinary things.

At last, after nine long, grueling weeks, I landed at the Los Angeles Airport. There my family was reunited to carry forth the traditions of love and life and happiness. Several weeks later we had wonderful news about Leila's medical condition. She was suffering from a severe case of rickets, which can be completely corrected through diet, vitamins, and exercise. We had been blessed again.

Through this experience, I have learned that love is larger than all the obstacles and walls that try to limit it. I have learned that love often requires extensive sacrifice and constant faith. Love was the ultimate power that allowed the gathering of these priceless lilies of God's field.

Sandi and Carly Lichfield

"UNTO ONE OF THE LEAST OF THESE..."

as told by
Sterling and Sandi Lichfield

"I wish I could say that I was craving another baby, but I wasn't," Sandi Lichfield admitted. "I was already a grandmother! I had five beautiful children of my own and three wonderful grandchildren." However, Sandi, who had spent years working with the Right to Life organization, watched three of the *20/20* programs about Romanian orphans and couldn't get them out of her mind. The neglect of these little ones touched her deeply. After watching the third segment, she turned to her husband, Sterling, and said, "Let's go to Romania and give at least one of those children a home."

Sterling had not watched the full program. The scenes were so graphic that he had had to leave the room. He could tell from the tone in Sandi's voice that she was serious about going to Romania, but he had challenges of his own to worry about. In addition to his responsibilities as the president of a large Connecticut stake, he also had employment concerns. Along with several others, he had recently lost his job when his employer made drastic cutbacks. He considered his alternatives: I am a grandfather and have lost my job; I can either stay home and play golf or venture to Romania. He finally said, "I am ashamed that I didn't think of it myself."

Sterling and Sandi immediately went to work completing the prerequisite legal papers. Because they were so confident about their decision, they were surprised by the opposition they received from nearly everyone they encountered. Most of their friends said that they were much too old to adopt a child; it was time for them to care for their own needs, especially now that Sterling had lost his job. Where would they find the money? Some Church members reminded them of Sterling's duties as stake president. How could he leave all his ecclesiastical responsibilities?

When Sterling went to get the required police clearance, the woman officer was enthusiastic about their adopting a child until she learned that he was fifty-four years old. Then she angrily lectured him for twenty minutes, repeating over and over that he was too old to adopt.

Even close family members could not understand their desire to adopt. One of their sons called on the telephone. "Mom, I don't want you to go," he pleaded. "I am almost thirty years old, the last thing on earth I need is a baby sister." The Lichfields, unprepared for so much disapproval, began to question their own judgment. Now, as they look back on the experience, they can see how, at the most crucial moments, God provided the very miracles needed to assure them that regardless of how others felt about their decision, he would support them.

One of those little miracles occurred as the Lichfields struggled to obtain the required funds. To make the trip they needed an extra $4,000. Without employment, they could not even apply for a loan. Sandi felt impressed to make it a matter of prayer, but Sterling objected. "That would be praying for money," he told her.

"I know," Sandi answered, "but if that is what we need to get to Romania, let's pray for it. If it is the right thing, and I think it is, we will get the money." Together they knelt and prayed that if God wanted them to go to Romania, he would help them find the money for the trip. The next day they were surprised to receive a check in the mail for $4,021 from Sterling's former employer for vacation time that he had earned but not used.

The opposition from others continued, but Sandi kept the picture of a little girl who had been adopted from Romania to help her through this difficult period. The baby had been featured in a magazine article, and Sandi had cut the picture out. She had even talked to the adoptive parents over the phone. Whenever she'd start wavering, she'd pull out the picture and look carefully at the beautiful child. The picture would always bring tears to Sandi's eyes. With renewed resolve, she would tell herself that she had to go.

In December, while preparing a special Christmas message to present in her Relief Society class, Sandi picked up the scriptures. As she opened them, they seemed to fall open to Matthew 25:

> *For I was an hungered, and ye gave me meat: I was thirsty, and ye gave me drink: I was a stranger, and ye took me in: Naked and clothed me: I was sick, and ye visited me: I was in prison, and ye came unto me.... Verily I say unto you, Inasmuch as ye have done it unto one of the least of these my brethren, ye have done it unto me.* (vv 35–36, 40)

Sandi blinked back the tears and read the scripture over and over again. It came alive with new meaning for her; the scripture was speaking directly to her about the Romanian children. They were strangers in a faraway land, hungry, sick, naked, and imprisoned by orphanage walls. She cried for a long time. When she finished, she realized that her heart had been changed. It was as though a complete metamorphosis had taken place. She was no longer timid, worried about what others thought. She had the answered prayer, the Romanian baby's picture, and now this scripture to keep her going.

The Lichfield's original plan had been to leave in March or April, but both Sterling and Sandi began to feel an urgency to leave for Romania as soon as possible. They purchased airline tickets for 2 January 1991, just as the Romanian airline went on strike. Four days later they were able to leave on the Yugoslavian airline, JAT. Although their luggage was 500 pounds overweight from donated supplies for the Romanian orphanages, airline officials agreed to carry the bags of humanitarian relief supplies without charge.

While on the plane, they met Garth and Carolyn Nelson, who were also traveling to Romania to adopt. They decided to stick together through the experience. It was a joy for them to learn how much they had in common with the Nelsons. Garth and Carolyn were also members of the Church and had older children. Carolyn Nelson and Sandi Lichfield looked almost like sisters. Tiny details about each of them were strikingly similar. They felt as if they had known each other for years.

In the course of conversation, Garth revealed that his father had died one week earlier. Garth's father had told them before he died that he would help them go to Romania. They thought he meant financial help, but after he died they realized that if he had lived, they would have never gone. He was so sick that they would have stayed home by his side.

The plane landed in Belgrade, Yugoslavia, during the Yugoslavian Christmas celebration. The pilot, anxious to celebrate the holiday, became too drunk to continue the flight to Bucharest. Airline authorities tried to get the 120 passengers to take a 36-hour train ride to Bucharest, but most of the passengers, having heard horror stories of robbery on that particular stretch of railway, insisted that the airline fly them the rest of the way. The airline relented and told the passengers to be ready to load at 6:00 a.m. the next morning.

The passengers showed up on time, but the plane didn't take off until 6:00 p.m. It flew halfway to Romania, then turned around and landed back in Belgrade. "Romania is fogged in," they were told. Finally, three days later, they were flown to Bucharest.

The two couples spent their first night in Romania in a hotel and ordered dinner in a restaurant. The food was so bad that no one could eat it. Instead they ate granola bars they had brought with them.

Early the next morning they walked to the American Embassy. Sandi thrilled at seeing the Eastern European architecture and tried to look at all the buildings. But after tripping over several potholes and landing flat on her face twice, she realized that it was safer to look at the ground when she walked. None of the streets had been repaired for years, and some of the holes were four to five feet deep.

The guard at the embassy asked Sandi how long she would be staying in Romania. When she answered that she planned on staying six weeks, he looked worried and said, "Too bad. War in the Gulf is about to break out and there are a lot of Arabs here." As predicted, the Gulf War began while the Lichfields were in Romania. It was very frightening to be an American overseas at that time, and news reports were hard to find.

The Nelsons and Lichfields hired a United States citizen who had been born in Northern Romania to be their guide. He agreed to take them by train to his hometown of Suceava to visit the orphanage there. The night was black and foggy when they arrived at the filthy train station. It was filled with sad-looking people with a gray tone to their skin. Most of them were obviously going without basic necessities.

When they finally arrived in Suceava, their guide loaded them and their nine suitcases into his tiny Romanian car. Most of the luggage was tied onto the top of the rickety vehicle.

When they asked him how old the car was he replied, "Next year it votes!"

The guide had arranged for the Lichfields, the Nelsons, and Vic, another American, to stay in an apartment which had been newly cleaned and painted. Russia could be seen from one of the windows. There was running water, and it was even heated, a luxury. Meals were to be provided for them, but this amounted only to one loaf of bread each morning for the five people sharing the apartment.

The Lichfields were told to get a good night's sleep, for they would be visiting an orphanage the next morning. There were two little girls in the orphanage that could be adopted. Vic, who would be arriving in the morning, had first choice of which girl to adopt. The Nelsons had to wait a few days before the guide could help them.

At nine o'clock the next morning Vic arrived, a big burly, bearded man of Italian descent. The Lichfields traveled with him and their guide to the orphanage, where they were taken to a very small room. A nurse was asked to bring in a baby girl, just six months old. From where she was seated, Sandi could see the baby being carried down the hall and into the room and knew it was her baby. But the nurse carried the girl over to Vic.

After what seemed like an eternity, Vic handed the baby to Sandi. As Sandi began to talk to the baby, the director of the orphanage and their guide began to cry. The Spirit filled the room and Sandi felt an intense bonding with the baby. As she handed the baby to Sterling, the same feeling overcame him. He knew she was their baby. He felt like running out of the building with her to take her immediately to America. But neither of them could say anything, as Vic had the first choice.

Soon the nurse came in with the second little baby girl, a perfectly beautiful baby. But when Sandi held her, the same feeling was not there. This little girl was just not their child, and they knew it. After playing with the second baby for awhile, they handed her to Vic. The big Italian-American bounced the baby girl on his knee. "Do you know what I'm going to get for you in America?" he asked her. "I'm going to get you some spaghetti, and some linguini, and some tortellini!" Then the little girl magically smiled at him. He looked deeply into her eyes and said, "O.K. I'll take this baby."

Sandi and Sterling were overjoyed. They tried to act calmly as they said, "That's fine. We are quite happy with the other baby."

Vic and the Lichfields spent the rest of the day in the orphanage nursery getting to know their babies. The baby Vic had chosen was nine months old. She already had a habit of rocking back and forth in her crib because there was no one to rock her. The Lichfields' baby had open sores on her body. They tried to get clean sheets on her bed, believing the dirty bed might be the cause of her boils. A few days later, after bringing gifts for the nurses, they were allowed to put clean sheets on the crib and clean clothes on the baby.

Watching the babies' bath was a shocking experience. The nurses dumped a bucket of ice cold water over the screaming babies' heads while scrubbing them hard with soap. Then they dumped another bucket of water over them to rinse the soap off. Afterwards they picked the babies up by the neck and carried them to a changing table; the nurses thought this was good for the babies' backs. Sandi was grateful when the nurses allowed her to give her baby a more gentle and loving bath.

The Polaroid camera they used to take pictures of their baby was a new adventure for the nurses. They all wanted their picture taken. Their faces would light up, and they would giggle as they watched the prints develop before their eyes.

Back at the apartment, the Lichfields showed a Polaroid snapshot of their baby girl to the Nelsons. "This is going to be our baby," Sandi excitedly told them.

"She is dressed in yellow!" exclaimed Carolyn.

"Well, yes," Sandi replied, wondering why Carolyn seemed so surprised.

Several times during the week Sandi heard Carolyn repeat to herself, "That baby was in yellow!" A week later when it was more certain that the Lichfields would actually be able to adopt the baby girl, Carolyn confided to Sandi, "I hope you are not offended but I think you need to know something. When we were on the train from Bucharest to Suceava, I knew you were going to get a baby, and I could see you with that baby, but the baby I saw you with was in yellow. I was concerned because you had brought only pink things." This was another confirmation to Sandi that she had found the baby meant for her.

It took ten days to finalize the adoption. During that time, Sterling became violently ill with both asthma and an allergic reaction to the extensive air pollution. Outside, the town was covered with a terrible cloud of smog, and inside was just as bad, because nearly all the Romanians smoked. The Lichfields had brought every medication they could possibly think of with them; but even so, Sterling's lungs literally shut down, and he became delirious.

At that time Sandi appreciated the fact that their Heavenly Father had them traveling with the Nelsons. Garth was a faithful priesthood holder and the Lichfields were able to ask him for a priesthood blessing for Sterling during his sudden battle for life.

After the blessing, Garth and Carolyn were inspired to seek help at the orphanage. They asked if they might possibly have any medication to help with allergic reactions or asthma. When the nurses learned that it was for Sterling Lichfield, they remembered the cases of supplies he had given them and were very glad to help. Miraculously, a few months earlier a group from Belgium had given the orphanage three inhalers. They gave one to Sterling, and it helped him breathe better.

For ten days Sandi divided her time between caring for Sterling at the apartment and caring for their baby in the orphanage. The sights, smells, and sounds at the orphanage began to wear on her; they seemed to grow worse every day. Each evening as she left, the thought of returning made her cringe, and she felt that she could never make herself return. Each new morning, however, the desire to be with and care for her baby gave her the strength to go back.

One woman stayed at the orphanage with her two-month-old baby, because she had nowhere else to go. She followed Sandi around constantly. On the third day the translator helped them to converse. The woman told Sandi that she could see that she loved children. When Sandi responded yes, the woman asked if Sandi could please adopt her baby, who was in the orphanage. Sandi did what she could to help, but the baby's father refused to sign the adoption papers.

During this time, Sterling remained critically ill. Knowing it would be cold in Romania, the Lichfields had packed two battery operated electric socks, and Sterling wore them around his neck. When he had to appear in court, he covered the electric socks with a scarf and was able to appear well enough that the judge granted the adoption.

Sandi wanted to name the baby Meagan. However, one day when she was alone, she heard the voice of her father who had passed away years before. "Sandi," his voice said, "there was a time when I would have opposed this adoption. But things are different now. You have done the right thing, and I am very proud of you. I would also be very pleased if you would name this baby Carly." And so Sandi named the baby after her father, Carl Alvord.

Their new friends, the Nelsons, were able to adopt two girls, ages four and seven. When they first went to the orphanage to see the girls, the seven-year-old kept circling them. She went to a worker and asked, "How do I tell them that I love them?" When they offered her candy, she said they should give it to the other children; there would be a lot of candy for her in America.

The Nelsons were not able to visit the girls during the two weeks while finalizing the adoptions. During this time nobody had told the girls whether or not they would be adopted, but the girls never gave up hope of going to America. After the adoptions were final, Garth came to the orphanage and took them out to a waiting cab. The youngest one looked up at him and asked, "America?"

"America," Garth answered, and the little girls began to cry with joy. Then Garth and the translator started crying. Even the cab driver, who had daughters of his own, began to cry. He had to pull off to the side of the road. It was a half hour before they could get going again.

When the Lichfields' adoption of Carly was final, they traveled to Bucharest, where they had to obtain a visa for Carly to enter the United States. Unlike their previous apartment, their room in Bucharest had no heat, and the temperature inside was chilly. They had no hot water, and the toilet seat was shattered. Carly was sick and Sterling's condition was rapidly deteriorating. He had severe diarrhea and had lost 40 pounds. The embassy was closed when they arrived, so they could only wait. It remained closed Saturday through Monday for the Martin Luther King holiday. Sandi was frightened and angry that she had to wait three days for the embassy to open. She spent the weekend watching Romanian news coverage of the Gulf War, not understanding a word.

When the embassy finally opened, they obtained the needed visa for Carly and began the journey back to the United States with their precious bundle. A worker in the Yugoslavian airport noticed the baby and commented, "You rich Americans. You just come right over and adopt these babies with no trouble."

"Don't you think that for one minute!" Sandi replied. "People are selling their cars and homes to afford this. Most have taken loans from friends and family members and sacrificed their life's savings. And to think it was no trouble. My husband nearly died!" The woman was surprised. It had not crossed her mind that those who came to Romania to adopt the children did so at great personal sacrifice.

At last they arrived back in the United States, where both Sterling and Carly were rushed to the doctor's office. In time, both recovered. Carly managed to grow six inches in six months.

In the beginning, the Lichfields had been surprised at the great opposition they faced, but as they returned home with Carly, they were even more surprised at the great outpouring of love for their new daughter. Family members and friends reached out for Carly and openly wept with joy to see her. "How beautiful," total strangers exclaimed. "We want a baby like this!" Sandi's mother's heart melted at the sight of her new granddaughter.

"How did you do it?" many have asked Sandi.

"I felt the Spirit so strong while I was preparing to go to Romania," she answers. "And while I was there it carried me and even pushed me right through all the hard times." The Lichfields have continued to face many challenges and trials. They are still unemployed, and their savings are depleted. But they are certain that they did the right thing. They know firsthand the joy that Christ spoke of when he said, "Inasmuch as ye have done it unto one of the least of these, my brethren, ye have done it unto me."

The Jolley Family

IF YOU'RE WILLING, I COULD USE YOU

Jeanna Jolley as told to Sherri Bird

December 1991 is the first anniversary of my Romanian odyssey. A flood of memories overwhelm me and evoke images of unspeakable joy and pain. The pictures in my mind are filled with Romanian faces. I see the people and their country; I feel their pain; I hear their voices and understand their struggle for life. Most of all, I see their children. I will never forget the children.

My husband, Lindsay, and I were married in 1978. In 1980 our daughter Kelli was born. After nine years we adopted our son, Devon. I had agonized about raising Kelli as an only child for a long time, and now it appeared that Devon would be resigned to the same fate. We wanted desperately to provide both our children with siblings to grow up with, but our avenues into adoption seemed to end in stone walls.

An article about a couple from Oregon going to Romania to adopt sparked our interest. We were hesitant at first for many reasons. One big barrier for me was the overwhelming idea that I would have to choose a child from a sea of many hopeful faces. It seemed too much like picking a puppy: "Yes, I think we'll take this one." How do you choose a child?

The breakthrough occurred when I was writing in my journal. I recorded:

> *These are Father's children. They are His. I can trust Him to set things right. If not in this life, then when they pass through the veil. I am only one person: I can only do what I can do. If that is only to love one of those children, then I'll do it! Then, almost like a voice, a message came directly to me from my Heavenly Father: "Jeanna, if you're willing, I could use you."*

At that moment, I was acutely aware of the lifelong commitment we would be making by adopting a child who might carry emotional and physical scars from a life of neglect in an orphanage. When Lindsay and I discussed our concerns, we were amazed to realize that we were more congruent with each other about this adventure than anything we had ever experienced. We were both absolutely convinced that this was Lord's answer.

Once we had firmly made the commitment to go, we next had to decide when to go. This seemingly small detail became a critical factor that affected the destiny of our entire Romanian adoption odyssey. We both felt an inexplicable urgency that I should leave on 1 November. The logistics of preparing to leave in such a short time, only two months, presented an incredible challenge. Nevertheless, we pressed forward and never altered that target date.

At first, we only planned to bring home one child, although it wasn't clear to me how old the child would be. Some friends pressured us to find a newborn—a baby would be less traumatized and bring home fewer problems. We never closed our minds to the idea of an older child, but we hoped for a baby. One Sunday in early October as I was writing in my journal, the idea came forcefully in a flood of tears that there were, in fact, two children waiting in Romania for us, a little girl and a baby boy. Even after this feeling came to me, I was hesitant to assign gender to these children. I bought generic clothing for the older child, not trusting my impression that it was a girl. However, much like the little boy who was the only one to bring his umbrella when the townspeople met to pray for rain, I knew I had to demonstrate more faith. I took the generic clothes back to the store and bought size four girl's clothes.

One of my greatest frustrations was the scarcity of information regarding Romanian adoption. I followed every lead I could get my hands on, many of which were dead-ends. But amazingly, one by one the stepping stones began to appear. Documents I had never heard of were obtained, certified, and notarized in triplicate. Ordinarily a home study requires months to complete; our home study was finished in three weeks by a caseworker who put everything else in her life on hold to complete it, motivated by a personal spiritual experience regarding our Romanian children.

Upon the advice of other successful adoptive parents, we decided to obtain enough donated medical supplies to fill a suitcase in the hope that these might be useful in obtaining entry to Romanian hospitals and orphanages. Local seminary students raised $2,000 in four days to help pay for medical supplies. Donated money also came from caring individuals who read an article in the local newspaper describing my journey. I was grateful to be able to use all the donated funds to aid the orphans. By the day of departure, we had 24 large suitcases full of medicine and supplies.

As we prepared for the journey, both Lindsay and I felt that I should be the one to go. He would need to stay home with our two children and work in our photography studio. However, when we told our parents about our plans, they expressed concern about my going alone, so my mother agreed to accompany me. We made arrangements for child care, and as I prepared to leave my family, I wrote:

I feel like the shepherd who left his 99 sheep to search for the lost one. I am leaving my two kids and my husband to search for my other two children. They are out there, my Romanian children. I love them already. I pray for my little girl, that she will feel comforted and have hope, that the flicker of a spark will not utterly fail before I get can there and rekindle it.

As 1 November drew near, anticipation nearly consumed me. When the plane finally lifted off, I was encouraged by the idea that this departure was much like our journey to earth from the premortal world—everything we do here helps us get back home to our heavenly parents. In much the same way, every step I took from this point on would lead me back home with my new children to complete our family.

After a 24 hour flight, we finally arrived in Romania. I should have been exhausted, but instead I was exuberant. Everything I saw was dark and dreary, a stark contrast to the inner radiance that filled my being. I felt full of inspired purpose and was eager to begin my quest. We loaded all the luggage into three tiny broken-down cars and maneuvered our way through town to a drab high rise apartment building. We could hear crowds demonstrating against the government two blocks away. All three cars drove right up onto the sidewalk, honking at pedestrians, who were not surprised to have to run for their lives.

The elevator, which barely fit three people, carried us only as far as the fifth floor. We walked up two more flights of stairs to apartment #72, which would be our home base for the next six weeks. The apartment was incredibly small. Our luggage completely filled the living room, and a small portable refrigerator stood in the hallway because there was no room in the kitchen.

My first experience with orphans occurred the next day. We had met a couple from Idaho, also prospective adoptive parents, who invited us to come with them to a hospital where they were following a lead. I recorded my first impressions in my journal:

> *As we walked down the corridors of the hospital, I had the feeling we were in an old, abandoned school building. We were met and refused entry by an aggressive, greasy looking woman who, to my horror, was named Gina! The interpreter argued with her for some time until we were permitted entry. I've tried for two months to prepare myself to view the horrors I knew I would see. The preparation helped, but I found myself clenching my teeth to hold back my tears and keep my fist from punching Gina's yellow teeth right through the back of her throat. She was embarrassed that we had come unannounced. The babies hadn't been tended to for hours. They were soaked. The rags that they put them in served as their diaper, clothing, and blanket. The air was hot and muggy in the rooms, about ten cribs to a little room. No toys, nothing but blank walls to stare at all day, every day, day after day after day. One little boy had been there two years. He propped himself up on his stilt-like legs, leaning on the crib rail, his haunting, sunken eyes and grayish skin betraying so obviously his keeper's neglect.The despair of these children was tangible to me.*
>
> *I could feel their devastation, their utter sadness. At one point I simply could not hold back the tears. I had wandered into a room with four babies, three of them tiny as newborns, though they were 3 to 6 months old. One little guy, swaddled up like an Indian papoose, had fallen sideways off his*

> *prop so that his face was in a pillow. He couldn't move anything except his neck. He could have being lying like that for hours, his plaintive cries unheeded. I gently rolled this urine-soaked bundle onto his back. As he looked into my face, I just bawled for the agony of it all.*

From the beginning, I clung to the belief that when I saw the children that were meant for me, I would recognize them. As I looked into the faces of all those children at the hospital, none looked familiar to me. I felt a deep compassion for these children, and would have liked to rescue them all, or at least pursue the adoption of one. But I felt a loyalty to the child that was meant for me, and though my heart ached for these small ones, my child was not there.

Looking back, I can see that certain events along the way were truly miraculous, though I didn't realize their importance at the time. In fact, many times I felt devoid of the spiritual guidance I had become so accustomed to feeling during my two months of preparation. I came to depend on my own determination and the memory of that feeling which had led me to Romania in the first place.

The significance of the 1 November departure date became clear to me in the Frankfurt airport when I met a man who introduced me to Juliana, my first translator. Before leaving, I had felt impressed to start looking for my children in Rimnicu Vilcea. Juliana's mother had a friend, Carmen, in Rimnicu Vilcea who knew the director of the orphanage there. Carmen came with us to the orphanage and convinced the director to allow us into the sleeping area where the children were napping. Ordinarily we would have been allowed no further than the foyer, and one child would have been chosen by orphanage personnel to be brought out to the foyer for us to view. Because I assumed that this would be a baby orphanage, I was shocked to find that all the children were between three and six years old. I was looking for my baby in Rimnicu Vilcea because I had an impression that I would find my older child in Satu Mare, a town far to the north. So when I saw that there were no babies here, I looked at the children with the hope of possibly finding an adoptable child for someone else. One child caught my eye as we walked through the room. Because all of the children had short hair and were generically dressed, I couldn't tell if this child was a boy or girl. Understanding our inquiry, an orphanage worker showed us that she was a girl. Several things about this child were striking. While some of the children held back in fear, this little girl seemed gregarious, even charming, as she smiled at us and laughed when my mother tickled her. I was curiously amazed that a child who had lived her entire life in an orphanage could have such spunk. We left, but I tucked her memory into a corner of my heart.

What should have been a one-day drive to Satu Mare took us three days in Juliana's rattletrap. Juliana's car was a typical Romanian putt-putt. We had a ritual we performed every morning to get the thing roadworthy. First, we'd squirt lubricant into the ignition and jam the key in. Then together we would crank the key to start the engine. If the engine didn't turn over, Juliana would take the windshield off and beat on the battery cables to get the connection going. The speedometer didn't work. We filled up with oil every time we filled up with gas. Some mornings the engine would catch fire, and finally the brakes went out. It took us two weeks, but at last we managed to kill Juliana's car.

I didn't realize that there were no highways in Romania. We had to travel across the country on these little back roads, all the while competing for space with cattle and oxcarts. When we got to Satu Mare, we visited all four orphanages, searching for my little girl. She wasn't there. We saw 400 children, and I didn't recognize any of them. I was devastated. I had been so certain that she would be there. I plummeted into deep despair and found myself wondering and doubting, frantic with confusion. All the way back I questioned myself, my motives, my reason for being here. A wave of loneliness engulfed me. Where were my stepping stones that had led me here? My darkest nightmare of having to choose a child randomly was looming ever nearer on the horizon. As we saw more and more children that I didn't recognize, the nightmare grew larger and larger until finally I couldn't run from it anymore. I turned to face that fear.

> *I knew this would be the hardest thing I'd ever done in my life, but I didn't know it would be because I'd have to choose. I thought the choosing would be done for me by a divine source, and I would just recognize the choice. All day long I've been working through this new idea of choosing. It's like I'm resigning myself to pain. Perhaps the Lord had to drag me to Satu Mare to show me that there are not just two children here all picked out for Jeanna Jolley—there are many children in Romania that I could love, that could be in my family. I have a gift of being able to bond with and genuinely love many children. The one that works out will be my child, and I will love it. I just realized that for the first time in a week, I will go to bed tonight in peace.*

At this point I determined that I would pursue the adoption of Loredana, the cute little girl we had seen in the orphanage at Rimnicu Vilcea. We were able to locate her birth father on a street corner in a small village 30 km away. We took Cornelia, the orphanage secretary, with us to help negotiate if needed. Initially Dumitru, the child's father, was unwilling to agree to the adoption, protesting that he wanted Loredana. But Cornelia argued that the birth mother would never consent to this, and that Loredana would be consigned to a life in the orphanage. Even though I couldn't understand their words, I realized he was saying no, and I was bereft. I knew Dumitru had never visited Loredana in the five years she had lived at the orphanage, and that he was not paying any child support. I began to weep, feeling this little life slipping out of my hands. In a sudden moment of inspiration, I pulled out a small packet of family snapshots and handed them to Dumitru. He looked at them slowly. A glimmer of warmth appeared in his eyes, as he chuckled at my daughter's Halloween costume and my toddler's happy face smeared with oatmeal. After several long, tense moments, he handed the pictures back to me. "Okay," he said quietly. He told Cornelia that in America Loredana would have a chance for a good life.

I was elated. Half this battle was won, or so it seemed. Now I had to find the birth mother and obtain her consent. But there was a serious problem: Juliana was wearing out, and her car was on its death bed. I had to find another translator. We went to a hotel lobby where I knew I could find adoptive parents. After two hours of networking I hired Marcell, a strikingly handsome, very charming man. We set off for Chirnogeni, a tiny village in the south by the border of Bulgaria. There we hoped to find Maria, Loredana's birth mother and convince her to come to Rimnicu Vilcea to release Loredana to me in court.

Marcell's car was no Romanian putt-putt. We made the six hour trip in less than four hours. Marcell knew exactly where to go to get information about the family, and in less than ten minutes we were in front of a little shack. A tiny woman dressed in rags was washing clothes in a bucket. A child similarly dressed was playing nearby with some rusty wire. When the mother looked up, I recognized her immediately. She had Loredana's face. She dried her hands on her apron as Marcell stepped out of the car and introduced himself. The contrast between these two people was startling—flashy Marcell was dressed to the hilt while this woman wore rags. But somehow the combination was exactly right, because these poor people were impressed by his obvious wealth and his warm acceptance of their meager existence. This was especially important, because Maria's present husband, Viorel, was the one whom Marcell had to convince, even though Viorel, in his traditional smallness of mind, would never accept Maria's child by another man.

It was obvious that Marcell commanded Viorel's respect, and after several minutes of discussion, Viorel brought out the kitchen table, stools, and his best homemade wine. Marcell warned us not to refuse whatever was offered us. We didn't have to drink it, but we should accept it graciously. So we sat there on stools in the mud, in front of the little shack they called home, holding the homemade wine as if it were the most normal thing in the world. I actually developed some compassion for this woman who had abandoned her child in the hospital immediately after the birth. Maria did what she had to do to survive the only life she'd ever known.

The next day, all of us piled into Marcell's sporty little car to make the eight hour trip to Rimnicu Vilcea where papers were processed, and the court date was set. Now all we needed was the judge's signature. I thought this would be a piece of cake, because everyone I had talked to who adopted from Rimnicu Vilcea had gotten the papers through the same or next day. But this was not to be. When we went in to see the judge, Marcell was his same proud, arrogant self. This demeanor had worked well with Loredana's mother, but the judge hated him, and Marcell would not back down. As a result, we had to wait eight days for the court date. Even worse, a new law requiring ten additional days when the birth parents could change their minds had just been introduced. Eighteen days seemed as long as eternity to me. Anything could happen. As we had gone back to visit Loredana, we had noticed foul-smelling drainage coming from her ear, and we knew she had a raging ear infection that wasn't being treated. Now it would be eighteen more days before she would receive any treatment. I felt angry and helpless. I begged Marcell to plead with the judge, but he refused. Although I feared that I would lose Loredana, I could do nothing but go back to Bucharest. Despondent and furious, I cried for a good hour on the way back. I wrote in my journal:

> *It feels like I'm being led around by a ring through my nose. I have to play their game according to their rules, but they keep changing the rules. Just when I think I'm going to get my arms around that child, someone comes along and grabs the ring in my nose and pulls me in another direction. The rules of the game change, and I have to follow the course or lose the game.*

Thinking that his work day was over, Marcell cheerfully assumed that we were going straight back to the hotel. When I realized this, I dug my heels in. The day wasn't over. I had eighteen days to wait, so we might as well use the time to find my baby. I ordered Marcell to stop in Gaesti at a hospital where I had previously seen a premature baby boy who might be adoptable but needed to gain enough weight to leave the hospital. Marcell grudgingly agreed.

When we inquired about the baby boy, we found that he was sick and couldn't be considered for adoption. While we were inquiring about other possibilities, a young woman wearing a hospital gown approached us and told us that she had a four-day-old baby boy that she would not be able to keep. As I grabbed that girl and hugged her, I cried some more. We went to see her baby, a scrawny little five pound peanut with a beak for a nose and a big brown birthmark in the middle of his face. I thought, "Can I love this baby?" I knew immediately that the answer was yes. The doctors assured us that the birthmark would fade in a year or so, and as far as they were concerned, he was a healthy child.

The next day Florentina, the baby's mother, garbed in her hospital robe, accompanied us across town to an office where we could obtain the baby's official birth certificate. We entered the little office where at first we were ignored and then yelled at. We waited a full 20 minutes for the clerk to finish her project, which was addressing, stamping, and gluing envelopes. The woman, who in my mind resembled the Queen of Hearts of *Alice in Wonderland* ("Off with her head!"), finally finished her project and turned her attention to us. Florentina gave her the name I had chosen for our son, Jaron, and requested an official birth certificate. The Queen spewed forth a tirade of Romanian, waving her arms and screaming. Marcell said the Queen didn't like the name I had chosen. It wasn't a proper Romanian name, and she flatly refused to fill out the birth certificate. Marcell argued with her for a few minutes and finally, in exasperation, we gave up and named him Mihai, a respectable Romanian name. This pacified the Queen of Hearts considerably, and she filled out the birth certificate in her very best handwriting, meticulously, fastidiously and with a practiced flair. It took her a full half hour to handwrite all the information twice—one for us and one copy for her. Finally we had the document and could proceed with the rest of the paperwork.

Jaron had not been gaining weight while Florentina was nursing him, so the doctor finally allowed him to have the formula that I provided. But Florentina was having difficulty getting some of the nurses to bring warm water to mix with the powdered formula unless she tipped them, and since she had no money, she couldn't always give him the formula. Consequently, Jaron did not gain the weight he needed to leave the hospital as quickly as we had hoped. When we realized this was happening, we gave Florentina money to tip the nurses so she could feed the baby.

At long last, Florentina and Jaron were discharged from the hospital. Since she was only seventeen, we needed to get her father's signature for the adoption papers. We drove to Gura Foii to get Gheorghe, Florentina's father, and bring him back to court. Even though Gheorghe feigned indifference and forbade Florentina to keep the baby, he wished his grandson godspeed and played a Romanian love song on his accordion for us. I somehow loved this crusty old man, who had the strength to combat his pain, blink back his tears, and go back to work. His life, like Maria's, was one of survival in a very hard world, but his courage and endurance still shined through.

On the day we took Jaron out of the hospital, another woman came to me with a child for adoption. Just the day before, I had met two couples at the American Embassy who had been in Romania for two weeks and hadn't seen a single child. They needed a translator, and we knew of children who were waiting to be adopted. The couples hired Marcell immediately. My work was basically finished. All that remained for me was picking up the paperwork from the judge in Vilcea and getting Loredana out of the orphanage, which couldn't be done for another week and a half. We breezed through Jaron's paperwork, completing everything in only six days.

During this time, I met a genuine man who spoke excellent English and told him the story of my adventure so far. I asked him if he would be interested in driving us to Vilcea to see Loree, the name we had begun to call Loredana, one last time before my mother left for America. We had been in

Romania five weeks, and she decided to go back as scheduled. I had to wait out the eighteen days to get Loree and finish her American paperwork. He agreed to drive us there and offered to speak to the judge to see if we could get Loree out any earlier.

I didn't expect the judge to treat him any differently than he had Marcell, and so didn't allow myself much hope that anything would change. But I couldn't have known that his gentle meekness would soften the heart of such a pompous man as the judge. Imagine my joy when the judge waived the remaining time and gave us the documents which released Loree from the orphanage. After distributing some well-placed gifts, we procured the rest of the documents we needed that same day, and Loree was ours.

We went to the orphanage to sign all the final documents. Loree knew she was going to come home with us, and so did the other children. She may have boasted about this to them, because the day before she left, a group of children attacked her, and we could see bruises and scabs from the beating.

It was a pleasure to peel off the filthy, tattered rags she had lived in for so long. I took out the clothing I had brought for her, and the witness of my faith came full circle as I slipped a little pink sweat suit on her small brown body. Everything fit perfectly. Loree was almost six, but she was a perfect size four.

I asked Loree if she wanted to say goodbye to any of her friends. Without a second glance, she said, "No! I never want to see them again. I want to go to America with Momica." I asked if there was anything she wanted to bring with her, but she owned nothing. She brought nothing with her from the orphanage but the scars on her body.

It was an incredible experience to communicate entirely by touch and pantomime. Loree slept in my arms all the way back to Bucharest. When she wasn't sleeping, she was drinking in all the physical and emotional stimuli she had missed for the first five years of her life. She had freedom to explore a world she had been shut away from, things she had never seen, heard, touched, or experienced in any form. It was a challenge to keep up with her curiosity, but there was a part of me that was unspeakably relieved to find this spark within her had not been extinguished.

After our return, I reflected on my experience in Romania and for the first time realized the miraculous connections that enabled each piece of the puzzle to come together. At the time, I was unaware of how significant each part was. For example, if I hadn't left 1 November, I wouldn't have met the man who introduced me to Juliana and subsequently to Carmen. Without Carmen's assistance, I would never have seen Loree. If Juliana had remained our translator, we wouldn't have met Marcell, whose charmingly arrogant manner was just the ingredient we needed to soften Viorel and harden the judge. Of course, the judge's resistance infuriated me, but if he had released Loree immediately I would never have found Jaron. Then my last translator entered the picture just in time to convince the judge to waive the rest of the waiting period. As a result of all this, we were able to leave five days later, sparing us further expense and enabling our family to enjoy our first Christmas together.

I learned a great deal from this adventure. When I didn't know what to do next and it seemed that everywhere I turned was a dead-end, the memory of my purpose in coming to Romania and the conviction to be there filled me with strength to keep going. I saw many good-hearted, loving people who would have been wonderful adoptive parents, but who gave up when the way seemed too hard. Often the risks were high, and the answer to the problem appeared imprudent or extravagant, even dangerous. But the bottom line remained: obstacles are what you see when you take your eyes off the goal. For me the risks became relative when the lives of my children were at stake.

Jordan Quigley

It Would Take a Miracle

Alicia Quigley

In April 1990, when I was five months pregnant with our fifth child, my husband Jim and I watched the first *20/20* segment on the children of Romania. I cried for hours. We wondered what it would take to get a child out of those horrifying, inhumane orphanages. Jim and I sincerely felt that there was a baby there meant for us.

A few weeks before our daughter Kilee was born, we watched the next report on *20/20* which showed the asylums for unwanted children. We knew then that we would have to find our baby from somewhere in Romania and bring him or her "home." We believed that no matter how impossible it seemed, there had to be a way to accomplish this.

When Kilee was two months old, we learned that a man in our town was in Romania adopting a child. I called his wife and told her of our desire. Because we already had five small children of our own (our oldest was six), she was surprised but told us how to get started. We completed the paperwork in December. As I hung Kilee's first Christmas stocking, I prayed that there would be an additional stocking or two to decorate our fireplace next year.

After much deliberation, we decided Jim would have to be the one to go to Romania. He had two weeks of vacation coming, and we hoped he could complete the adoption during those two weeks.

Three days after Jim arrived in Romania, new adoption laws went into effect. Although he tried, none of the orphanages would let him in. He needed permission from the new Adoption Commission in Bucharest. That week Jim met a Romanian man who understood the adoption laws and was willing to help him.

Private adoptions were still allowed, and the man told Jim about a baby boy named Claudiu who lived with his teen-aged mother in a small farming village. The woman's husband had abandoned her when she became pregnant. The father claimed the child was not his and filed for divorce the day Claudiu was born.

Jim found Claudiu and his mother in a tiny shack with neither plumbing nor electricity and only a small wood stove which served for both cooking and heating. The dirt floor was damp, and icy cold winds blew in through the cracks between board walls. Claudiu was wrapped in a tattered blanket. His mother was feeding him water with a worn nipple pulled over an old brown pop bottle. There was no food in her house and it appeared that water was all she had to keep him alive. Claudiu was nine months old but was only the size of a new-born. He had a terrible cold. In spite of being ill and severely malnourished, he smiled when Jim held him and instantly won Jim's heart. Jim promised Claudiu's mother he would do everything he could to adopt her son. Claudiu's mother felt it was the only hope for the child's survival.

Jim went to work on the adoption. To his dismay he learned that Claudiu was not eligible to enter the United States because two parents were listed on his birth certificate. Only children with one parent on the birth certificate could receive visas, unless they had previously been abandoned by their parents. We appealed to our senators, the State Department, and to embassy officials. Everyone seemed sympathetic, but none could help. Immigration authorities could not give this starving child a chance to live even though his father had filed an affidavit with the court officially disowning him. We could not adopt Claudiu. By then, I loved him as if he were my own. He was so sick that I wondered how he could survive much longer. My heart still aches for him. I have asked others traveling to Romania to check on him for me, but none have been able to find him.

Jim spent the next week working on the adoption of a baby girl. The mother seemed to like Jim and agreed to the adoption, but his hopes were dashed again when he arrived at the courthouse to begin the paperwork, only to learn that the parents had decided to give her to a couple who offered them money for her. Precious time had been lost, but even worse, we lost the little sister we were hoping to find for our Kilee.

Jim was now on leave without pay, and we still had no prospects of finding a child, let alone completing an adoption. We feared Jim would have to return home empty handed. That week an envelope surprisingly appeared on Jim's desk at his office. Inside was an unexpected $500 bonus which gave us what we needed for Jim to stay in Romania one more week.

By this time, Jim had made friends with several other Americans in Romania. One woman told Jim about Tudorel, a baby boy she had seen in the orphanage where she had found her baby. Tudorel was nine months old and had been there since birth. She told Jim that Tudorel was wrapped up like a mummy, his arms secured firmly across his chest. His wrappings covered him completely except for a tiny square which allowed his mouth, nose and eyes to peek through. She said that as she bent down and began to speak to him, he smiled. She hoped that somebody could adopt him, and after two hours of pleading by her interpreter, she had been able to get the names of his parents from the orphanage.

Jim and his translator went to meet Tudorel's parents to ask if they would consent to the baby's adoption. When the mother saw Jim, she looked surprised. "It is you! You are the man from my dream. You are the one who has come from America to adopt my baby." She explained that the night before she had seen a man in a dream, and she knew he was a good man. She saw his whole family in the dream and knew this was where her son was supposed to go. She felt it was a loving family, and her son would have a good life with them. When Jim showed her a picture of our family, she became excited. We were the people she had seen in her dream.

Two months before, she had been approached by another couple who wanted to adopt Tudorel, but the father did not feel right about it and absolutely refused. Now that they had met Jim and because of the mother's dream, both parents were anxious that Jim adopt Tudorel.

Jim still needed the consent of the Adoption Commission to enter the orphanage to see Tudorel and gain the necessary documents. On Monday, Jim and five other Americans went to the Adoption Commission. Normally Jim would not have been granted an appointment, but because the other five in his group had appointments and because Jim's request had been in for two weeks, he was allowed to speak to an official. He was told that the Commission would give approval if the orphanage would send a list of their children as written proof that Tudorel was in the orphanage.

On Wednesday Jim waited three hours at the orphanage to speak with the head nurse. At first, she tried to discourage Jim by saying Tudorel was going to be adopted by his uncle. Jim knew better, so he requested birth and health certificates for Tudorel. The nurse said she would not give them to Jim unless he brought approval from the Commission. The Commission told Jim they would not give approval until they received the required documents from the orphanage. However, they did agree to officially request a list of children from the orphanage. Jim went to the Commission daily to see if the list had arrived. Even though it would have taken the head nurse only ten minutes to fax the information, she steadfastly refused to do so.

Meanwhile, Jim did all else possible to hasten the adoption. He filed Intent to Adopt papers and completed a required home study on the birth parents. He was even able to secure a court date. But time and money were running out. Jim had been gone for three weeks. The judge could not approve the adoption without the Commission's approval. The Commission could not give approval until the head nurse relinquished the appropriate documents. The head nurse at the orphanage held the key, and it appeared she was purposely trying to obstruct the adoption.

The next Monday Jim again went to the Commission. The Commission official agreed to call the orphanage. The head nurse answered the call and claimed that she had no adoptable children. When pressed for the truth, she finally admitted that Tudorel was on their list of children, and she said she would send the list of children. We were suspicious of her true intentions but hoped the documents would reach the Commission in time for our court date.

The next Wednesday Jim wrote in his journal:

> *I can't believe we have come this far to fail. The list didn't come again today. Tomorrow my interpreter will go to the orphanage and not leave until he has a letter for the Commission. This gives me hope, but it means that we will not have the Commission's approval for our court date tomorrow.*

At court the next day a member of the Church had her appointment right before Jim. The judge read through her home study and was very surprised. “Three children! You already have three children and you’ve come all the way around the world to get another child?”

Her translator quickly stood up and told the judge about Mormons. “Mormons believe that their family is the most important thing to them. They love lots of children and believe that they are the greatest blessings in life.”

Jim came into the courtroom next. The judge read our home study and slowly looked up from the bench. “Five children!” he said. “You have five children? Let me guess, another Mormon?”

The judge allowed Tudorel’s birth parents to complete their part of the adoption so that they would not have to make the trip into town for court again, but he could not finalize the adoption until we brought the Commission’s approval. He scheduled a second court hearing for a week later.

After court, Jim and his translator went straight to the orphanage and told them they would not leave until they had documents to give to the Commission. The head nurse absolutely refused to document that Tudorel was inside. In a heated conversation, she revealed to them the reason for her behavior. In January, a couple from Canada who wanted to adopt Tudorel had offered a large sum of money to the orphanage director and the head nurse to be able to adopt him. However, Tudorel’s birth parents were not willing to give the couple their consent. Because the nurse and the director did not receive the promised money, they became very angry with Tudorel’s parents. To spite them, the head nurse swore that she would never allow the child to leave the orphanage. She admitted that she would do everything in her power to prevent the adoption.

Nothing they could do would convince the nurse to change her mind. Jim was numb with disbelief. That night, when I spoke with him, we cried for a long time. There was no time for him to begin a new adoption; he needed to get back to work as soon as possible. I made Jim promise to visit the

Commission one more time before he left Romania. We would pray for a miracle. I felt that Tudorel, or Jordan, the name we had given him, was meant to be ours. The tiny boy we had never seen had forever become a part of our lives. We knew it would take a miracle to free him from the vindictive inhumanity of the head nurse and the orphanage director.

The next morning Jim packed his bags to come home. Before leaving, however, he went one more time to the Commission office. It was officially closed on Fridays, but since he had promised me to make every effort, he went anyway. The official who had been helping him was there. Jim found out that she had felt so sorry for him that she had been to visit a very high official in Romania to tell him Jim's story—how he came every day for news from the orphanage. She told the official that she had received verbal confirmation that Jordan was there, but the nurse had refused to send the list. The man's heart softened, and he gave her permission to approve the adoption without the list. Jim was told to come Monday to pick up the official approval.

Our miracle had happened. Jim was so ecstatic that he ran all the way to the apartment and called me. It was 2:30 a.m. when the phone by my bed rang. I picked up the receiver and heard Jim's voice on the other end screaming, "We got him, Dear! We got him!"

Sunday night, Jim received a blessing from the elders of the Church. They were not allowed to help in the adoptions in any way but were wonderful at giving moral support. In Jim's blessing, he was told that he would get his baby, but it would take longer than we had hoped. As it turned out, the uncaring attitudes and hard hearts of people we still had to deal with would complicate the process and cause many problems and obstacles that we had yet to encounter. At the time, it was hard for Jim to imagine what else could possibly go wrong, but we had the comfort of knowing we were doing what the Lord wanted and that he would help us through it.

On Monday he was able to get the approval of the Commission. He clutched it tightly and kissed it as he left the Commission office for the last time. He made copies and headed straight to the orphanage. When he arrived, the nurse had no choice but to give him the birth certificate. But even though she had thought it was impossible for Jim to get the Commission approval, she was taking no chances and had sent Jordan away. Under pretense of illness, she had sent him to a hospital in Bucharest. This also gave her sufficient excuse to refuse to issue the certificate of health we needed to complete the adoption. She thought that since Jim had never seen Jordan, he would give up. We feared for Jordan's safety. When Jim arrived at the hospital in Bucharest, it was closed. The next day he received confirmation that Jordan was inside, but he had been placed in the Infectious Disease Center with very ill children. Only nurses were allowed inside this unit. Strangely, the hospital officials agreed to issue the certificate of health needed for our court date the following Thursday.

Jim was in court on Thursday with everything he needed to complete the adoption, but the social worker who did the home study on Jordan's birth parents didn't show up. We were shocked that someone would be so careless with employment being so scarce, but we later found out that she was a friend of the head nurse. Court was rescheduled for the following week. Again we faced what seemed like endless days of waiting and disappointment. If Jim could just have been allowed in the hospital to see Jordan and be there with him it would have been much easier to wait.

At home I thought people were beginning to tire of hearing me say that Jim would be home "next week." I wondered if this would ever end and if he would still have his job when he returned. I was grateful to my family and friends who were supportive and caring, and who took the time to listen while I poured out my troubles and frustrations. I spoke to Jim daily and framed a copy of our $1,001.23 phone bill.

When court convened the following Tuesday, the social worker was present, but she had purposely not obtained the mayor's signature on the home study that had been done on Jordan's birth parents. Furiously, the judge sent the prosecuting attorney from the court to the mayor's office. The mayor agreed to call a special meeting of his social committee to sign the document instead of waiting for their usual Monday meeting. The judge told Jim to return Friday to finish the adoption. Court was not usually held on Friday, but the judge made this exception.

On Friday, the home study was signed, and at 1:30 that afternoon, Jim received the final decision. It was the opinion of the court that the adoption be granted. The birth parents of our new son were in court that day with Jim, as they had been for every court hearing. They had to ride the bus in from the country where they lived. When they knew the adoption was final, they were at last content.

At home, sound asleep, I was awakened by Kilee, who let out an unbelievable scream. I ran to her bedroom. There she was with the biggest smile I had ever seen, squealing with delight while she jumped up and down. Then she plopped down onto the mattress and started clapping. "Babies are so weird," I thought. "Doesn't she know it is 4:30 in the morning?" When I called Jim the next day, I learned that it was the exact moment that he had received the adoption decree.

Jim immediately made the three-hour trip to Bucharest to pick up Jordan, but the nurses said it was too late; patients were never released on weekends. He would have to return on Monday. We were extremely disappointed; Jim had been in Romania more than six weeks and still had never seen Jordan. We had so hoped he would finally be able to hold him, now that he was ours. Again we would have to wait out the weekend.

At home I began to prepare for their homecoming. I put blue balloons all over my front yard, and hung up a huge banner that read, "It's a 16 pound boy!" Then I began to mow the lawn. A woman stopped to ask if I was mowing the lawn for the poor woman who had just delivered a sixteen pound baby. "No, I am the woman," I replied. "and my husband delivered him." Another passerby asked if the mother survived the delivery. "She almost didn't," was my honest reply. Later we learned that we had over estimated the quality of orphanage food. Jordan, who was now eleven months old, weighed only fourteen pounds.

On Monday morning Jim went straight to the hospital. The director said that Jordan had to be sent back to the orphanage; Jim would have to pick him up there on Tuesday. We were terribly disappointed and worried again for Jordan's safety. We hoped that on Tuesday Jim would finally see the face of the little person for whom we had fought so hard.

On Tuesday we heard a rumor that the workers in the orphanage had been threatened with losing their jobs if they tried to prevent us from getting Jordan. It may have been true, because the head nurse brought Jordan out to Jim, but only after what seemed to be an eternity of filling out required forms. When the nurse handed Jordan to Jim and he looked at the little round face with huge brown eyes, he was grateful he hadn't given up.

On the long ride back to Bucharest, Jordan sat on Jim's lap. He pressed his little nose up against the window and stared in amazement at the world outside the orphanage. It must have overloaded his senses, because before long he was fast asleep. Our littlest son had finally begun to live the day he turned eleven months old and his Daddy held him for the first time.

Some time later, when Jim was back at the apartment, a neighbor stopped by to see the baby she had heard so much about. The woman, totally by coincidence, bore an uncanny resemblance to the head nurse of the orphanage. When she came into the room Jordan shook with fear and started to scream. He refused to look at her and clung tightly to Jim. We can only imagine the treatment Jordan must have received at her hand. His arms still bear the scars of his life in the orphanage.

Jordan had been wrapped like a mummy for nine months. He had never learned how to sit up or how to use his arms or legs. His ribs were misshapen because his arms had been strapped so tightly to them. Freezing conditions in the orphanage had caused water pipes to burst, and the resulting swamp beneath the cement floors harbored swarms of mosquitoes. Jordan looked like he had the measles because of all the bites on his face.

By Friday, Jim had assembled all the papers necessary for his visa interview. The day was long for Jordan, who was going through withdrawal from the narcotic sedatives he had received in the orphanage. They waited outside the embassy in a long line for an hour, in order to be admitted when the visa window opened at nine. After Jim turned in his papers, he waited two hours for his name to be called. Jordan was very uncomfortable. Not only was he going through withdrawal, but both his ears were both badly infected. An embassy worker came out to the lobby and asked Jim to take the crying baby and leave. Jim had no one to tend Jordan while he waited for the visa, so he replied that if she gave him a visa, not only would he leave, but he'd never come back.

Just before noon, Jordan was issued a visa to enter the United States. Their flight home was going to stop in Germany, so Jim also needed to obtain a German stamp for Jordan's passport. The German Embassy closed at noon. Unless he could get there before they closed, Jim would have to stay another week before there would be another flight home. He hailed a taxi and dashed across town. A man was just locking the doors to the German Embassy as they pulled up at exactly 12:00 noon, but he was kind enough to let them in. Jim was ecstatic when the German official quickly stamped Jordan's passport. They were free to come home.

Our entire extended family was at the airport to welcome Jim and Jordan home. They looked great to me, and we probably looked pretty good to them too. I looked into Jordan's beautiful brown eyes and told him I was his mom. I told him he had four brothers and a sister who loved him very much. The two months of anguish had been worth it. Our family was finally together.

Jordan has grown and changed in so many ways it's hard to list them. He runs around the house on never-tiring legs and befriends everyone he meets. He does everything in a hurry, as if to catch up for lost time. Jordan also gives the sweetest, wettest kisses. Sometimes he can't hug hard enough to let you know how happy he is. He and Kilee especially are "best friends." He's learning to talk now too, and his little voice sounds so sweet when he says such simple things as "mama," "dada," and "hi!" And Jordan loves to sing. He sings the cutest little jabbery songs ever. He dances to anything that has a beat, including the busy signal of the telephone and the singing in church. Sometimes it's hard to maintain a quiet reverence in our church meetings because Jordan is standing on the bench, rocking out to the songs. Our particular favorite is entitled, "Because I Have Been Given Much," for we recognize that God blessed us beyond measure when Jim came home from Romania holding our son, Jordan, in his arms.

Kristina and Lisa Larsen

A TIME FOR GROWTH

Ginger and Chuck Larsen

Patience may be my biggest challenge. I want everything now. I guess my Heavenly Father knows this too, and he loves me enough to help me develop this valuable trait. Thirteen years ago I went through a very painful temple divorce. I had two small children and wasn't trained for a career. Many times I prayed and asked, "Why? What do I need to learn from this?" In my search for an answer, I visited Temple Square in Salt Lake City. I walked through each room on the lower level of the Visitor's Center. As I was about to enter the last room, a voice came to my mind, saying, "If you enter this room you shall receive the answer you have been seeking. Are you strong enough?"

At the time the room was full of paintings which portrayed the hardships of the early Saints. Two pictures in particular caught my attention. One depicted the Saints being driven out of Missouri. There was violence in the background, and a woman with long red hair, much like my own, was in the foreground. One small child clung to her legs, and she held another in her arms. Terror filled her eyes. The other picture showed some of the Saints crossing the plains in the cold and snow. The voice came to my mind again, saying, "Someday, Ginger, you'll have challenges as great as these. If you do not have challenges like the ones you are going through now, you will not be strong enough to overcome the challenges that are to come."

I spent the next thirteen years trying to convince myself I could never endure such trials. I hoped that the Lord would let me avoid them. Now I am grateful that a loving Heavenly Father knew that with his help, I could endure this great challenge.

Just before Halloween 1990, my husband, Chuck, and I were overwhelmed by news reports that documented the legacy of Ceaucescu's communist regime in Romania. Thousands of children suffered untold horrors in overcrowded Romanian orphanages. Five of my cousins from California left for Romania to adopt two or three children. For fourteen years I had desperately wanted to have another baby, and I longed to go with them, but we had just built a big new home and money was very tight. To help make ends meet I was operating a very large preschool. Adoptions were taking from four to six weeks. We would encounter mountains of paperwork and bureaucratic red tape. There would be so much we would have to take with us—medicines, food, diapers, formula, etc. It all seemed impossible.

After my cousins left for Romania, I could not sleep at night or think about anything else. I knew I had to go too. I asked my friend Kerry if she and her husband Leonard would consider traveling to Romania with us to adopt children. Kerry's reaction was like mine—sleepless nights and a sense of urgency, so we decided to approach the Romanian trip as a common goal.

We were told over and over that we could not possibly leave before the end of January, but I miraculously found people whose schedules allowed them to substitute in my preschool. One by one we managed to overcome all of the other problems as well. As we boarded the plane for Romania on 1 December, we knew that with God, nothing is impossible. Even so, I did not realize what an emotional trial this experience would be.

The cold, dimly lit airport in Bucharest looked like the rest of Romania; it was impossible to tell whether it was being built or being torn down. Everything seemed dark, colorless, and ill-maintained. Policemen were everywhere as though they were an occupying army. Machine guns rested on their shoulders, and pistols hung at their sides.

After resting from the long flight, we began our search. Kerry and Leonard were assisted by a couple named Tudor and Margarite. A man named Serban helped Chuck and me. Serban's English left a lot to be desired, and we were often very confused and frustrated. The first few days seemed long, cold, and discouraging. But every day something happened to lead us to our babies, though we didn't realize it at the time.

Tuesday was our first day of actually looking for children to adopt. We drove from one village to the next, checking hospitals and orphanages. Finally, the director at one orphanage agreed to let us in. The doctor at the orphanage showed us two little boys. One of them, Mihai, was two years old. Chuck and I had already decided to adopt two little girls, but Mihai's large brown eyes, curly eyelashes and cute smile melted our hearts. We both wanted to adopt him.

We found Mihai's birth father at the end of a small valley in a very tiny village. I was devastated by his response. He would not consent to Mihai's adoption. He looked upon the orphanage as a very convenient full-time day care center. He thought there might be a chance to get Mihai out in a few years when "things got better."

In a few years! Obviously he had no idea what orphanages in Romania were really like and the effect that environment would have on his child. It totally devastated us to leave Mihai, but without his father's consent, we had no other choice. I thought my heart would break in two. I cried the entire three-hour ride back to Bucharest. My faith began to waver and I wondered, "What if we can't find the child for us?" We still talk about Mihai—cold, alone, and hungry. We still long to give him the love and nurturing he hungers for.

When we returned to the apartment, we compared notes with our roommates. They had found a nine-month-old baby boy near Focsani they thought we might be interested in. They had arranged for their driver to take us to see him the next day.

When we went to see the baby boy, I was so afraid of going home with empty arms I made up my mind we were going to adopt him, no matter what. As I played with him I said to Chuck, "Well, what do you think?"

Chuck did not feel like this little boy was meant to be ours. His reply sent pains through my heart. "He's OK, but I really think we should try to find two little girls." I knew then that the baby boy was not my child and that we would have to keep looking. How could I hand him back to the nurse after wanting a child so desperately for fourteen years? It was the most painful moment for me in Romania. I left the orphanage broken-hearted.

Later that day we found a three-month-old baby girl near Buzau, but were told to come back the next day to see if she was still available for adoption. Kerry had hoped to adopt a little girl near there, so she went with me when I returned. I was disappointed to learn that the three-month-old baby's aunt had decided to adopt her. I knew it was probably the best thing for the baby, but the fear returned that I might have to go home empty handed. Perhaps I was just there to help Kerry find her children.

As we drove across town to work on an adoption for Kerry, we each prayed silently that at least this one would work out. Kerry and Leonard had both felt strongly that this baby was theirs. They were eventually allowed to adopt her, and we shed many grateful tears.

On the way back, as we passed through Buzau, I asked if we could stop and check out the Buzau maternity hospital again. We had been there before and were not in the habit of going back to the same place, but I felt we should check this place one more time. A little boy had been born that morning, and the mother had left right after he was born. We got her name and address from the hospital staff, but they thought she might have given them false information. We found the village, but no one there had ever heard of her. I was getting discouraged, but Leonard agreed to stop at the hospital the next day to see if they could find a correct address for her.

That night I called one of my cousins who had come to Romania shortly before I did. I was frustrated because before we had come to Romania I had been told about two premature baby girls that were available. I wanted to go see if they were still there, but the woman who told me about them had misspelled the name of the town, and I could not figure out where it was. My cousin said, "Oh, I talked to her too, just before she left Romania, and I have the name of that place written down here somewhere." She found it and gave me the name of the town. I was excited; I knew we should pursue these two babies. Now we just needed to persuade Serban to take us there.

Serban was a mechanic by trade, and one of his customers had told him about a premature baby girl who was in a hospital in Bucharest. He had talked to the hospital staff, and they had promised to let us have the first chance of adopting her when she was strong enough to leave the hospital. He took us to see her, but the doctor said she was too sick; they wouldn't let anyone see her for a couple of days. Serban didn't have any other plans for the day, so I immediately told him, "Take us to Pucasa! There is a maternity hospital there with two premature girls we need to find."

After driving for an hour, Serban became confused by his maps and unsure if he had taken the right road. He stopped in a little village named Racari to ask directions. The townspeople didn't know the way to Pucasa but told Serban that we should check for abandoned babies at the Racari hospital.

A tall cement wall surrounded the grounds of the Racari hospital. We drove through an iron gateway and down a narrow dirt driveway lined by tall scraggly trees. The sky was overcast and it was drizzling. On our left stood the gray, cheerless cement hospital. Behind it were several unheated bungalows for older children. I could feel the pain, loneliness, and death that existed there. Even though it was winter, the front doors were wide open. Dogs wandered freely in and out of the building.

After being told that only one baby under four years old was available for adoption, we were led to a room with a dozen white-painted, rusting iron cribs. Eight or nine babies filled the room, all of them about two years old. They each wore the same one-piece pajama. None had diapers. They lay in wet beds and a strong stench of urine permeated the air. The babies didn't even cry; they had apparently learned that it would bring no response from the nurses.

The little girl they showed us was two-year-old Elena. She had light brown hair and hazel-green eyes. I asked if I could hold her, and tried to pick her up. She began to scream, as though she were scared to death. I tried to calm her, but she became even more upset. The nurse said that because the children were never taken out of their cribs except for an occasional ice cold bath, they were afraid to be picked up.

I put her back in the crib. A very small young woman entered the room, and Serban explained that it was Elena's mother, who worked at the hospital. She had heard someone was looking at Elena and seemed excited that somebody might adopt her little one.

We got back in the car, and while Serban found the way to Pucasa, Chuck and I discussed our concerns about Elena. She was very cute, but seemed to have many emotional problems. We were not sure if we could take on such a challenge.

At Pucasa we learned that the premature babies had already been adopted; however the doctor at a second hospital in Pucasa showed us a beautiful eighteen-month-old baby girl with brown eyes and dark brown hair. I loved her instantly. I picked her up and played with her. She laughed and giggled. Her response was a delightful contrast to the one I had received from Elena. This little girl's name was Sperunsa, and she was exactly what I had hoped for. Excitedly, I told Serban to find out what we needed to do to adopt her. He left for a few minutes while I held her and cooed over her. Shortly he returned with bad news. "I'm very sorry. A man was here just two hours ago who has already decided to adopt her. But this one-year-old over here is available." I had to set Sperunsa down and go across the room to look at the other little girl, but it was no use. Sperunsa watched me sadly, as if to say, "Why did you leave me?" I couldn't stand it. I walked out into the hall and cried.

It had been a long, discouraging day, but on our way out of town we stopped at one more orphanage. The staff let us in and showed us a beautiful little boy almost four years old. I picked him up and bounced him on my knee. As I studied his face I realized that he looked just like Kerry's daughter, Amanda. I knew Kerry and Leonard would want to adopt him. We told the director that our friends would come the next day to see him. As we arrived back at our apartment, I could hardly wait to tell Kerry and Leonard about the boy. "I found Amanda's brother!" I exclaimed.

Meanwhile, Kerry was trying to tell me something exciting. "You won't believe what happened when Leonard asked the Buzau hospital if they had heard from that mother who abandoned her baby boy. They didn't have any news about her, but they said there was a one-week-old baby girl whose mother had asked them to find a family for her baby! We told them you would be interested!" I couldn't believe it. Was I dreaming? Could it be real? We found their little boy, and they found our baby girl.

The next day, Saturday, Serban took us on the five-hour round trip to see the baby girl Leonard had located for us. To our disappointment, no visitors were allowed on weekends. On Sunday Kerry asked Margarite, her golden-tongued interpreter if she would try to get us in. She agreed, so we all piled into the car and made the long journey again. Margarite asked the others to stay in the car, but took me up to the door of the Buzau hospital. It was locked. Undaunted, she led me around to an open side door. We went in through a kitchen and down a dim hallway until we found a nurse. Margarite talked her head off. She kept chattering and gesturing with the nurse until she led us up the stairs and down the hall to a nursery where a lovely little baby lay in a white metal bassinet. The doctor unswaddled her to show me she was indeed a girl.

The baby was placed in my arms. Her huge gray-blue eyes opened so wide you could see the white all the way around the iris. I held her close and fell instantly in love. She looked just like my daughter Sherri at that age and seemed to be one of my own. The fourteen years of waiting, the trip, the looking, the heartache were all worth it.

Margarite, who had been chattering away with the doctor, suddenly announced some good news. "The doctor is very kind; she wants to know if you would like your husband to come in and see the baby."

"Oh, yes! Please!" I responded. By then the baby was beginning to fuss. As soon as Chuck entered the room, however, she stopped to study his face with her wide-eyed look, as if she were seeing an old friend. We didn't know it then, but this was to be our Kristina Lee.

We still hoped to adopt two baby girls, but that night we were told that the sick baby in Bucharest was much worse, and the hospital would not let us adopt her. "Chuck," I said, "we must go pursue Elena in Racari."

"I know," he replied. "I feel it too." We didn't feel we were financially or emotionally capable of handling Elena's many problems, but we both knew that we had to go back to the gloomy hospital in Racari.

The long ride the next morning was silent. We were both apprehensive. The hospital seemed even more ominous this time, but we went in and asked to see Elena. When I picked her up she screamed even louder than before. I put her down and played with her for a moment. Then I turned to Serban and said, “Please go get started with the paperwork.”

He left the room for a short time and then came back and asked us to follow him. He said a woman had stopped him in the hall and asked if we would please look at her baby. We walked only six feet down the hall and into a tiny room where three small babies lay. Serban pointed to a tiny swaddled girl with several bonnets on her head. She was two months old, but weighed only seven pounds. She had dark eyes, and lots of dark hair peeked out from under the bonnets. Her skin was pale—she looked like a tiny porcelain doll.

I told Serban I was sure we could find a good home for her, because I knew several other people who were looking for a baby girl. He answered, “You don’t understand. You cannot have Elena. She has problems with her hips and will require much therapy. The doctor will not release her for adoption and is upset that someone led us to believe that she could be adopted. But you can have this baby.”

For some reason this news seemed perfectly natural, like a missing piece of a puzzle suddenly falling into place. I studied the baby’s face for a moment. She had tiny, delicate features, so perfect, so precious. I asked Serban to start the paperwork. Surprisingly, the baby’s mother reached into her purse and pulled out all the major documents we needed. Collecting the necessary documents for adoptions was usually a formidable task. This mother had obviously been watching and waiting, hoping someone would come and adopt this baby which she could not afford to feed and care for.

We worked for several hours and then returned to the hospital. I ran in to see the baby again. It was then that I realized how much I hadn't noticed before; when I picked her up, she was wet. None of the babies we saw wore diapers or plastic pants. She was swaddled in a piece of what looked like a rough woollen army blanket. Her bed had a stack of rags and half a loaf of old bread on it. The sheets were stained and soiled. Her face was dirty, and her nose clogged and caked with dried mucus. I pleaded with Serban to get the hospital to release her so I could take her away immediately. He said they were treating her for something; she was too sick to be released. How could I leave her in that dirty bed? Then a peaceful voice inside me said, "It will be all right. She has survived for two months; she can survive another few days."

As we headed back to Bucharest we talked about the babies' names and felt that this dark-haired baby was definitely our Lisa Marie, and the light-haired baby in Buzau was Kristina Lee.

On Tuesday we went to get one-week-old Kristina out of the Buzau hospital. The nurse was sullen. She refused to use any of the cute baby things I had brought. She swaddled Kristina with two receiving blankets and a quilt. Then she gave me a glass baby bottle full of tea. Once outside, I cuddled Kristina tightly. It suddenly all seemed very real.

On Wednesday, we went to pick up Lisa. I could hardly wait to take her away from that gloomy hospital. The birth mother undressed her and seemed embarrassed because there was lint, dirt, and weeping sores under her arms and behind her ears. I didn't know if she had ever been given a bath. She surely didn't look like it. The mother tried to wipe off the puss from under her arms with a rag, but Lisa screamed. I motioned to her and said reassuringly, "It's okay. Don't worry about it." Of course she did not know English, but she seemed to understand and stepped aside to let me dress her. The women in the room stood watching and giggling. They had never seen cute little baby clothes before. Lisa's mother seemed pleased. Then she gently pushed me aside and showed me how to swaddle Lisa the

Romanian way, on top of the things I had already put on her. I watched and thanked her, realizing that this was the last thing she could do for her baby. She picked her up and placed her in my arms. Then putting her face down close to Lisa she spoke softly to her in Romanian and gave a last loving goodbye.

As I left, I noticed Elena's mother, tears streaming down her face. She was disappointed that we could not take her baby. What could I say? How could I comfort her? I walked over and put my free arm around her. She threw both her arms around me, and we cried together.

Three days later, Chuck and Leonard left for home to be with our families for Christmas. Kerry and I stayed to finish the last of the paperwork.

Over the next three weeks I felt the terror that I had been forewarned of thirteen years earlier. Romania was particularly unstable because it was the one year anniversary of the Romanian revolution. There were protests and strikes almost daily. Food shortages were common, and it was often unsafe to be out working on our adoption papers. Gas shortages threatened to delay us indefinitely. Civil war could break out at any time. In spite of my fear, I knew Lisa and Kristina were depending on me. In turn I had to have faith in our Heavenly Father.

On Christmas night our toilet clogged. Kerry and I put on some rubber gloves and went to work. It took several hours to take care of the problem, but we felt afterward that it probably was a blessing, because it kept us laughing and joking instead of crying. We missed our families terribly and wished we were home enjoying Christmas with them.

The last of our Romanian paperwork was finished 26 December. I then realized I had a major problem: Kerry had received clearance from United States immigration officials to apply for visas for her children, but I had received no word, even though our applications had been submitted together. What could have happened? I was able to get a message to

Chuck that my clearance had not come. If it didn't come soon, Kerry would have to go home without me. I would be left in Romania all alone with my two babies.

One afternoon I started getting severe abdominal pains. All the muscles around my stomach went into spasms. If I laughed or cried, the pains became extreme. I knew I couldn't get medical help. Fortunately, Leonard was flying back to Romania that night to bring supplies. By midnight he and one of the branch leaders were at our apartment giving me a priesthood blessing. As soon as they laid their hands on my head, the pains started to diminish. I was able to go to sleep, and the pains never returned.

Sherri, my teenage daughter, had called me on the phone earlier that day. I could tell she had been crying, even though she was trying not to show it. Then she brightened up a bit and said, "Dad just walked in. He's back!"

"Get on your knees and thank Heavenly Father," Chuck said when he took the phone. "Ginger, we've had a miracle today." He had just returned from Salt Lake City. Immigration officials told Chuck that they hadn't sent my clearance because our fingerprints had been lost. We would have to resubmit them, and I would have to wait in Romania for the eight to ten weeks it would take to clear them through the FBI in Washington D.C. While he was waiting to see a supervisor, Chuck silently prayed, "Heavenly Father, you've gotten us this far, and we really appreciate it, but we have done all we can do. Ginger just can't stay there for another eight weeks. We need some help here, please!" In a very rare move, a local clearance of our fingerprints was authorized. Our embassy in Romania would receive my clearance by Thursday.

The clearance did not arrive at the embassy by Thursday morning, but to keep calm I kept telling myself that in a short time I would be home making fudge with my family. I had asked Sherri to obtain all the ingredients. I wasn't craving the fudge; I was craving the happy times I remembered making it with my family as we all stood around with our "tasting spoon," talking and laughing and having fun together.

When I checked later at the embassy for my clearance, it was in a stack of cablegrams that had just arrived. The American and Romanian governments would finally allow me to go home! However, the Romanian airline was on strike. No one knew how long we could be stranded. Leonard had already left with the baby girl they had adopted, so Kerry and I decided we'd have to take a bold step. We would take her four-year-old Michael and my two babies on the 14 hour night train to Belgrade, Yugoslavia. Our Romanian friends told us this trip would be very dangerous. We were told not to sleep and to beware of thieves. It was not exactly what I had hoped to hear, but I knew the Lord would help us.

We felt very calm on the train, as if someone were watching over us. A very nice Italian man fell in love with little Lisa. He took us under his wing, and everyone else assumed we were with him. I believe God placed him there for our protection.

When we were asked to produce our passports at the Yugoslavian border, we realized that Michael's exit visa was missing. It is mandatory to produce that document when leaving Romania. A very intimidating soldier took all our papers and disappeared for a few minutes. When he returned, he handed us the packet of papers and let us cross the border. We were accustomed to experiencing miraculous things and breathed a sigh of relief.

At Belgrade we were able to get tickets on a flight to the United States for the next day. As we landed in New York I reached over and grabbed Kerry's hand. We both cried. Sixty-two hours after we left Bucharest, we landed in Salt Lake City. It was wonderful to have our babies safely home with us and out of the unrest and uncertainty we had left behind.

Chuck later summed up his feelings. "I thought we were just going over there to see if we could find a kid or two that needed a home, but it was not like that at all. We were led to these two babies. They are our children—there is no doubt in my mind about that."

A kind, patient Father in Heaven led us, protected us, and brought these beautiful little babies into our home. We are not only grateful for them, but also for the things we learned from this experience. Having faith doesn't mean we can move mountains whenever we feel like it; it means we can do it if it is Heavenly Father's will. Having faith takes patience and great inner strength.

Now I'm grateful I had to wait 14 years for more children; otherwise, I would not have Lisa and Kristina. Whatever pain and disappointment I endured was well worth it. Before I went to Romania I owned a successful preschool business and a large new home. Now my business is about half of what it was, and we will have to sell our beautiful home. But these things mean nothing when compared to what is really important to me: my faith, my family, and my precious little angels from afar.

Aurelia's adoption became official nearly two years after she was found in an orphanage in Bucharest.

The Shumway Family

(Cristian is pictured on his mother's lap.)

OUR FATHER'S WILL

Sam and Traci Shumway

The summer of 1980 marked my fifteenth year and the beginning of a very important mission for me. At the time, my family lived in San Jose, California. I had the unique opportunity of performing with the "Prunehollow Choral Society," a youth group named after the famous San Jose prunes. Our finale and highlight of the year was performing and touring throughout the beautiful country of Romania. I checked out books, articles, magazines—anything I could find about the history and culture of Romania. I bought a language textbook and started to teach myself Romanian. The more I learned, the more I fell in love with Romania. In my social studies, English, geography, and world history classes I chose Romania as the topic for all my oral and written reports. I began to live, think and breathe Romania. Many of my classmates thought it unusual that I became so obsessed with a country I had never seen.

At last, filled with excitement for the trip and gratitude for the financial sacrifice of my parents, I left for Romania with my performing group. We changed the name of our group to "Tinerii Californiei," which in Romanian means "California's Kids." We thought it would go over better with the Romanian people than "Prunehollow."

When we arrived in Bucharest, I felt like I had been there before. As I walked down the cobblestone streets and spoke with the Romanian people, a sense of familiarity overwhelmed me. My love for the country grew and grew.

While in the city of Sibiu I had a near-fatal accident. My life was spared only through divine intervention. During the incident I had a deep spiritual experience in which the Spirit told me that I had a special mission to fulfill in Romania, and that I would return sometime in the future to fulfill that mission. The feeling made such an impact on my young heart that I promised to live worthy of such a mission, whatever and whenever it was to be.

I was certain that I had a proselytizing mission in store for me, but one year before I was old enough to serve a mission I married my high school sweetheart, Sam Shumway. However, the awe-inspiring impression I had received lingered, and I knew that someday I would return to Romania. Perhaps Sam and I would serve a couples' mission.

We had our sons Taylor and Spencer very close together. Spencer was born with a cleft lip and cleft palate. Sam and I knew immediately that this was not just a happenstance, but rather a special gift and blessing from God. Later we we were to understand its full meaning.

On 5 July 1988, when he was exactly two months old, Spencer underwent his first corrective surgery. I was worried about this tiny child under anesthesia and the surgeon's scalpel. Never before had I felt so concerned. As I uttered one of many prayers in behalf of the surgeon and my son, a blanket of peace came over me. I was comforted by what I felt was not just one spirit, but many spirits. The thought came again into my mind that this beautiful boy had been sent to our family for a divine purpose, and that he was willing to take a less than perfect body in order to prepare us for what would come in the future.

The surgery proved successful, and both our boys continued to grow and bless our lives. We felt very strongly that there was another child was preparing to come to our family, and the feeling grew stronger and stronger. However, years passed without another child being added to our family, and at times we became very discouraged. Yet whenever we prayed, we felt that a child would be coming to our family soon. After several surgeries and many tests, my doctors were confused by my inability to bear children. By this time, we were very confused why Heavenly Father would give us the desire for another child.

While we were having all these mixed feelings, wonderful friends and family would do their best to console us by saying, "You can always adopt in the future." Sam and I came to the conclusion that if, over a period of perhaps ten years, we were still unsuccessful in having children, we might consider adoption.

On 14 January 1991 I finally reached my limits of patience and understanding. I was so consumed by the desire for a child that I became miserable, and my misery began to affect my family. I knelt down and pleaded with my Heavenly Father, "Please lift this pain from me. If we are to have a child, then let it so be. If not, bless me with understanding and strength to accept it. If we are to wait longer for a child, then please bless me with patience."

Never before had I such a frank and honest conversation with my Heavenly Father. I finally put my life and future into the Lord's hands; I promised that whatever his will was, I would accept it and live worthy of it. A sweet calm flowed through my body and mind. I knew my Heavenly Father loved me and all would be well.

That day I received an answer to my prayers. I drove past an anti-abortion display at a very large intersection outside the mall where we had been shopping. A sign said, "Honk if you love babies!" The entire intersection was full of honking cars. I was overcome with emotion. My four-year-old Taylor looked at the posters of aborted fetuses and said, "Mom, we would never do that to a baby, would we?"

I assured him, "No, we never would." Suddenly I had the desire to save one of those lives. I found myself wanting to convince women who would choose abortion to give up their child for adoption instead. I would be willing to adopt a child if it would prevent an abortion.

A half hour later I was waiting in the office of the surgeon who had just performed Spencer's third surgery for his cleft palette. To pass the time I usually read a pile of Dr. Seuss books to Taylor and Spencer. But this time I was particularly drawn to a magazine on the table. I picked it up and sat down, not knowing what was inside. It fell open to an article entitled "Saved by Love." A warm wave of spiritual confirmation came over me as I read. The article was about five families who had recently returned from Romania after successfully adopting children who had been abandoned in orphanages. I read about children who had been so neglected that at two years old they couldn't walk, talk, feed themselves, or even sit up. They could only rock themselves for consolation in their tiny cribs.

After I read the article, the whole room seemed to spin, my pulse raced, and tears flowed. I had a personal spiritual revelation that I needed to return to Romania to adopt a child. This was the mission for which I had been told to prepare eleven years earlier when my life was spared in Sibiu, Romania.

In less than three hours after my fervent plea to my Heavenly Father, my answer had been made known. I began making phone calls the moment I got home. My mother knew Ginger Larsen who had recently returned from Romania with two adopted babies. After several calls, I was able to reach Ginger. We talked for nearly three hours.

At first Sam was a little surprised, but by the end of my conversation with Ginger, he knew that we should look into a Romanian adoption. That night we marveled at the whirlwind of recent events. Only two days earlier I had confirmed to a relative that adoption would be a decision we would make far down the road.

Two days later Sam and I attended a meeting for those interested in adopting from Romania. I became convinced that we needed to leave immediately; there was absolutely no time to waste. I felt impressed to prepare and submit our papers promptly, although Sam wanted to wait until the fall so we could gather the necessary finances.

Because nobody adopting in Romania knew beforehand the child or children they would adopt, we had to travel to Romania to locate these children. The next evening, Ginger helped us get started. Without any knowledge of my own son's medical history, she informed me that children in Romania who had correctable problems were being overlooked. I felt a twinge of goose bumps as she told me of some of the deformities—crossed eyes, club feet, cleft lips and cleft palates.

She did not need to say anything else. That instant I was again overcome with the same powerful, almost exhausting, spiritual and physical prompting I had experienced earlier that week at the mall intersection, the surgeon's office, at home on the telephone, and at that meeting in Salt Lake. I could clearly see how the pieces of the puzzle were starting to fit together. Sam and I knew that we should pursue the adoption of a Romanian child with these special needs.

In three and a half weeks two other women andI received our clearances from the Immigrations office. All three of us experienced frantic feelings that we left for Romania two days later.

We arrived in Bucharest on Sunday, 24 February 1991, just 41 days after I had received the spiritual promptings in the surgeon's office. The next morning we set out to locate our children in the local orphanages. In a Bucharest orphanage I met and fell in love with Aurelia Nicolae, a bubbly, beautiful little girl two and a half years old who was born missing fingers on her right hand and missing her left foot. I immediately felt a strong desire to adopt her, but at the same time I felt compelled first to try to locate a child with a cleft lip and palate. My clearance gave me permission to bring home only one child.

In the days that followed, we found many cute, adorable children who all needed homes, but we did not find a child with a cleft lip and palate. My translators told me that they would be very surprised if we were to find such a child. Determined to follow the promptings that had been with me over the past eleven years, I continued my search. Meanwhile, I thought a lot about precious Aurelia and how much I wanted to bring her home.

Many people have asked, "How do you know when you see the child that you are to adopt?" Well, we weren't sure exactly how we would know, but we prayed fervently that when the time came, the Spirit would tell us.

Four days later, our translators felt impressed to travel to a small town located halfway to the Black Sea. As usual, they left us in the car and entered the orphanage to speak with the directors about any adoptable children. They soon came out and excitedly told me of a child with a cleft lip and palate. Another wave of goose bumps came over me as we walked into the orphanage and up the stairs to the office.

There, limp in a worker's arms, was a beautiful child wearing a pink sleeper and a pink bonnet, with wisps of light brown curls falling down its neck. I rushed to the worker, swooped the child into my arms, and looked into its huge expressive eyes. They told me the name of the child was Cristi. I thought she was the most gorgeous little girl I had ever seen. It was quite a surprise when they told me Cristi was a boy. Try as I might, I couldn't see a boy in all that beauty.

When I embraced Cristi, the same powerful spiritual feeling came over me that I had felt before many times. I could not stop talking. I was so excited; I kept saying, "He's the one!"

The next day, Friday, 1 March, we awoke early and drove a great distance to find the mother and the father to obtain permission to adopt their child. With them along, we waited outside the orphanage for my translators to ask permission for us to enter. Entrance into the orphanage was critical in order to obtain the release of information on Cristi necessary for his adoption. The orphanage director would not let us in at first because of an early morning announcement that the Romanian government had just passed new legislation which closed the doors of all orphanages to prospective adoptive parents. The director made a special exception only because we had seen Cristi the day before. The reason for my frantic feeling to get to Romania immediately became clear. Had we waited until the next flight, we would have arrived too late.

All through the adoption process I could see the hand of the Lord guiding me, my translators, and the Romanian officials. I have to admit that there were some difficult times, but through the power of the priesthood and in answer to fervent prayers, doors continued to open for us.

Perhaps the greatest challenge occurred when a certain official would not agree to the adoption. Although all the other authorities agreed, this man refused. Disgustedly, he questioned why I would adopt a handicapped child when there were plenty of healthy children from which to choose. I showed him a letter from the plastic surgeon in the States who agreed to perform the surgeries, photos of the hospital where the surgery would be, a letter signed by both Sam and me of our intent to adopt a child with a cleft lip and palate and raise this child as our own, and even pictures of our own son, Spencer, who had been born with the same deformity and whom we loved. We explained that we only desired to do the same for another of God's children.

Try as I might, this man would not relent. He feared what people would think of Romania if they heard that a handicapped child was adopted. After many prayers were uttered, the man's assistant, at the risk of losing his job, agreed to sign the papers. I am very grateful to this man and pray the Lord protected him.

On 12 March 1991, Cristi became part of our family. When I read his final adoption decree from the court, I learned that he was born on 5 July 1988, the exact day that our little Spencer underwent his first surgery to repair his cleft lip. The feelings of spirits comforting me in the hospital waiting room were preparing me for this mission. I know now that Spencer chose to take an imperfect body so that we would have the desire to bring another child into our family with the same need. We would have never considered such a thing had we not been given the experience with Spencer. We are convinced that Spencer and Cristi must have been great friends in the premortal world.

As I write this, a year and one month have passed since our return from Romania. We thrill each day with the progress that our son Cristi, whom we call Cristian, makes. Upon our arrival home, Cristian was very withdrawn. He was nearly three years old, but behaved as if he were only six weeks old. He had been fed only rice-milk and sugar, and he weighed only sixteen pounds. He was dehydrated, weak, and starving.

For his entire life Cristian had lain flat on his back, and the back of his head had conformed to the shape of the crib mattress. He had never rolled over onto his stomach, although he could rock violently from side to side when upset or tired. Every bone in his body protruded through his thin, pale skin. He could not even support his head well.

I had to hold him as if he were a tiny infant. He had never learned to sit up. His legs were severely atrophied and had no muscle tone. His knee caps had never formed the tissue and cartilage that allows the legs to lock and support themselves; thus he could neither walk nor stand. His eyes had not learned to focus on anything but his hands. They intrigued him, because that was all he had to occupy himself for the first 33 months of his life. He didn't know how to swallow or chew. When fed, he would gag as if he were drowning. He refused to be held for more than a few seconds and would go into a tantrum when cuddled. Cristian functioned in most areas as an eight-week-old infant.

His therapists were not sure he would ever be normal, but we knew our Heavenly Father wanted us to love him for who he was without knowing the prognosis. Within the first week of being fed formula, Cristian gained five pounds and began to take on a more healthy appearance. He soon underwent the necessary surgeries to repair his cleft lip and palate.

While observing him, we noticed that he did not respond to sound. Auditory tests revealed that due to chronic, untreated ear infections, Cristian had no hearing in his left ear and only a small trace of hearing in his right. We had tubes placed in his ears to allow the built-up fluids to drain. He now responds to every sound and covers his ears when the vacuum is on.

Thirteen months later, we can look back and see that Cristian has developed his motor skills as if he were born on the day he arrived in America. He learned to roll over relatively soon after our return, and with daily therapy from us and weekly therapy from a specialist, he slowly began to develop muscle tone in his legs, stomach, and back. He sat up around five months after the adoption as most five-month-old infants. Seven months after the adoption, he began to combat-crawl, also following the normal chronological time clock of a child of the same age. After ten months he pulled himself to a standing position, supporting his weight on furniture. The greatest event happened exactly one year from the day we adopted Cristian. On 12 March 1992, he took his first steps away from furniture on his own. He is now walking, at times staggering or falling, but walking, and he is as proud of it as we are.

Due to his hearing loss, Cristian had never learned to speak. For a long time all he would do was snort, grunt, or wail. We began to wonder if he would ever speak. Now after one year, he babbles. The sounds he makes are similar to those of a ten- or twelve-month-old baby. We are encouraged that he will someday speak, but realize he will need first to go through all the phases of development.

Cristian now thrives on attention and will let us know if he is not getting enough. At first all he wanted was to be left alone. Now he giggles, laughs, coos, and initiates interaction with us. He is particularly fond of Sam and would climb on him all day if allowed.

We have experienced many challenges since he came into our life. He was not a cuddly, sweet little baby that was easy to smother with love. We loved Cristian, but it took an enormous amount of patience to deal with his emotional tantrums and fits. It is interesting that our Heavenly Father would bless us with the very same challenge that, at one time, we felt we could never handle. The joy and rewards of this journey, the satisfaction of loving and nurturing one of our Father's children, have far outweighed the challenges we have faced.

Sam and I are convinced that nothing is impossible if it is the will of our Heavenly Father. He will never give us more than we can endure, as long as we remain faithful and do all we can to follow him. We are eternally grateful that our Heavenly Father was patient with us and saw in us a great potential. We have learned that as we completely put ourselves in the Lord's hands, with faith never wavering, all things are possible. Never before has our faith been tested to such an extreme, and never before have we needed to turn so much to our Heavenly Father for wisdom and comfort. We have been blessed to have developed the relationship with our Heavenly Father and our Savior Jesus Christ that came from going through these challenging experiences.

Sam and I also learned that every decision we make throughout our lives is critical. As we look back on the time that has passed since my experience in Sibiu, both of us faced decisions where one choice could have had serious consequences and the other led us down the right path to prepare us for our mission. Because of the guidance of wonderful parents and teachers, along with a continued relationship with our Heavenly Father, we were ready when we had to make difficult decisions.

Now, in answer to our continued prayers, the doors seem to be opening at last for us to bring another child into our family. We have been working on adopting precious little Aurelia, the little girl who was born missing her foot and some of her fingers. We know that if it is the Father's will, it will be so.

Editor's note: The adoption of Aurelia Nicolae became final in October of 1992. By the time the adoption was granted, Aurelia was four years old.

Alina and Alexandra Richardson each at three years old. They came to America when they were fifteen and eighteen months old, respectively.

With God Nothing Is Impossible

Holly Richardson

"I've just got to go to Romania," I thought as I sat nursing my newborn baby and reading the latest news reports. My son, Michael, had been born just twelve days before Nicolai and Elena Ceaucescu were executed in December 1989. Stories of Ceaucescu's legacy, tens of thousands of children abandoned in orphanages throughout Romania, had given me a tremendous desire to go to Romania and adopt some of those children, who otherwise might not know the love of a mother and father.

I always wanted to help and love children. Miraculously, I met and married a man who felt the same way. Greg and I had been married for four years and had three children of our own. During a twenty-one month stay in Washington State, we opened up our home to foster children. One little girl was with us for over a year, and it nearly broke our hearts when we had to let her go, even though she was returning to her birth mother who had undergone a dramatic change to get her back. We knew then that adoption was the way for us to be able to have a child forever and ever.

As I sat nursing my baby, I also thought of all the impossibilities of going to Romania. Greg could not leave his new job for that long, and I could not imagine going by myself. We were buying our first house, which used up all of our available money. I had just started a new job that

I loved, teaching prenatal classes for expectant mothers, and my three young children still needed me very much: Aaron, who had just begun preschool; Elizabeth, who was born severely handicapped; and baby Michael. I put Romanian adoptions to the back of my mind, but I did have a home study done "just to be ready," and began to earmark the earnings from my part time work for "Romania."

In December of that year, Greg was flipping through the TV channels and happened to catch the *20/20* segment which showed some of the adoptions that were taking place from the Romanian orphanages. I watched and cried. The Spirit testified to me that I needed to get to Romania. After the show was over and I was able to talk, I told Greg my feelings. I knew I had children over there who needed me. He looked at me through his own tear-filled eyes and said, "I know."

We were finally on the path of action; it was no longer a far-off dream. Going to Romania consumed me practically every waking moment. I felt an incredible urgency to get there and I came to realize that I would have to go without my husband. The thought scared me, but I finally reached a point where my children-in-waiting were more important and much more compelling than my own comfort.

About one month later I learned of a small group of women who were also going to Romania to adopt. I wanted to go with them, but they were leaving in less than a month. The next three and a half weeks were the most hectic ones imaginable, as I rushed to complete the mountains of paperwork. Of the five women in the group, only three of us were able to leave on such short notice.

Like most adoptive parents, we wanted to take relief supplies to the orphanages. To put together many supplies so quickly was difficult, but we were given a few donations, and I was able to purchase many items. I also tied about 15 quilts to add to the collection.

Our plane left early Saturday morning, 23 February. To be honest, I tried to leave home without saying goodbye to my sleeping children, but Greg suggested that I do so. When I walked into Mikey's room to say goodbye, I started to cry. I had nursed him one last time the night before; it was so hard to leave my baby. I cried most of the way to the airport, at the airport, and all the way to Denver. Aaron and Greg also cried as they accompanied me to the airport.

I was comforted to know, however, that I was doing the right thing. The night before I left, with the help of our home teacher, Greg blessed me that I would be able to find the children our Heavenly Father had prepared for us. The blessing gave me a wonderful confirmation that we did, indeed, have children waiting.

Getting to Romania was a two-day adventure. We slept off and on, as we could, whenever exhaustion over took us. The sight of heavily armed guards at the Bucharest airport was frightening, as were the intimate pat-downs at security checks. Our drivers were waiting for us outside the airport, and we soon learned that Romanians do not drive like Americans. When we asked where the seat belts were, our driver just laughed and pointed to a small hand grip above the door. I used that grip many times during my stay in Romania, especially going around corners at breakneck speed. We were dismayed to learn that our Romanian apartment had no telephone. Our families would have no direct way to contact us, and we could call them only through special arrangements.

Over the past months, I had considered adopting a handicapped child at some point in the future and felt that my daughter Elizabeth had prepared me for this. When I was finally through the major portion of the grieving process that takes place when a child is born severely handicapped, I realized that not only did I love and cherish her, but that handicapped children really weren't that scary or overwhelming to care for. I began to feel that we would be adding handicapped children to our family via this adoption, which I don't think I would have even considered without Elizabeth. I even started telling people that if I could choose a handicap, I would choose Down's syndrome, because Down's syndrome kids are always happy and loving. However, at the beginning of this trip, I planned on adopting two healthy, non-handicapped girls.

The first morning after we arrived in Bucharest, our agent took us to visit the handicapped section for younger children in a nearby orphanage. I noticed a playpen with about five children in it. Two of the children had Down's syndrome. Impulsively, I asked our interpreter for the day if they had any babies with Down's syndrome that were available for adoption. In the next room I was shown a small baby girl with sparse, white hair. As I picked up little Alexandra, my heart started to race and I thought, "I think this is my child." Alexandra looked and felt like a baby of perhaps six or eight months, but she was actually sixteen months old. I later learned that her birth mother knew I was the one to adopt her daughter immediately after she was contacted about it.

As we left the orphanage, I wanted to adopt Alexandra, but had not yet made a firm decision. After all, she was the very first child I held, and I didn't know if I would feel that way toward all of them or not. I was overwhelmed to realize I had the sole responsibility of finding our children. What if I couldn't hear what the Lord was trying to tell me?

Over the course of the week, I thought and prayed continually about Alexandra. From the phone center downtown I called Greg to ask him what he thought about bringing another handicapped child into our home. He said it was fine with him; he knew that whatever children I chose would be the right ones for our family. By week's end I knew I was going to bring Alexandra home with me. However, knowing Alexandra belonged in our family and actually bringing her home were two different stories.

The day after finding Alexandra, I continued my search to find a sister for her, but hospitals and orphanages had received a decree from the new Adoption Commission and would not let us in without Commission clearance. Accordingly, we went in to make appointments with the Commission to obtain clearance. We were devastated to learn that we could not get an appointment for nearly a month, which ended my hopes of being home in three to four weeks. That Saturday we phoned our husbands and told them that we weren't eating well. The next week they sent over a huge box of supplies with some acquaintances. The box contained 250 pounds of MRE's (Meals Ready to Eat), canned fruit and vegetables, puddings, Tootsie Rolls, cheese, and crackers. The day it arrived was better than any Christmas. I was sure I'd never stay long enough to need all that Greg had sent, but I was wrong. By the time I left Romania, I had only one small plastic bag left over.

On Sunday, we were able to go to church where a small group of missionaries and investigators were holding testimony meeting. I bore my testimony and expressed the heartache I felt at seeing children whose families could not take care of them, but who would if they could. I witnessed that Heavenly Father loves all of his children everywhere, and his heart must ache to see some of them living in conditions such as we'd seen. I felt thankful that the true gospel had been restored so that I could have my family forever. That conviction made it easy for me to adopt a child with a handicap, because I knew that one day, just like my Elizabeth, she would be perfect. That same evening I received a blessing from the branch leader, Brother Price, in which he promised me that I would find my second child within two days.

The following Wednesday we were allowed to return to an orphanage we had visited before the Commission's clearance was required. Even though it had been three days since my blessing, I knew that this was where my child was, as our contact had arranged our visit on Tuesday. We hoped we could locate the children we were to adopt and obtain the Commission's approval at our 18 March appointment. The workers brought in a few children for us to see, one or two at a time. The very last one brought in was a cute, chubby little girl with dark hair and eyes. Alina, just one month past her first birthday, was smiling and happy. After I told our translator that I would like to work on adopting her, the confirmation came that the decision was right. That same day, we set out to find her family.

We located Alina's seventeen-year-old birth mother, Daniella, in a small village, living with her mother and her mother's live-in boyfriend. Alina's grandmother was thrilled to consent to the adoption. Daniella did not seem to have very much to say in the whole affair, but went along with her mother's excitement to have Alina adopted. It became quite clear that the birth of the baby had been a major source of embarrassment for the family. They had even moved after the baby was born and had told no one in their new community about Alina.

We tried to file the necessary papers at the Tribunal, or court, for Alina's adoption. To do so, we needed to obtain documentation that Alina was actually in the orphanage. The social nurse for the institution was reluctant to provide it. She did not want any children adopted from "her" orphanage. After a full week's delay and lots of prayers, one of our translators was able to get the necessary paper from the orphanage. Then, when we went to the Commission to turn in the documentation, our translator had a heated argument with the top Commission official. Most of the people helping me were sure I'd lost Alina because of it. I was devastated, but I told myself to remember that God could clear the way.

On Monday, 18 March, the day I had my official appointment with the Adoption Commission, I was scared to death. I had spent so much time praying, I hardly had time for anything else. When I finally went to the Commission office, my stomach was tied up in knots, but my mind and my heart were at peace. I simply tried to have faith and kept telling myself that all things are possible for the Lord.

At the Commission office I was called in to speak to the same official who had been in the heated argument with my translator. I think she was testing me, because she asked if I had been in before. Remembering her fury the previous week, thoughts of lying momentarily crossed my mind, but I replied that I had been in the previous Thursday, and apologized for the confrontation. She looked directly at me and said in English, "Yes, I remember you very well!" Honesty is always the best policy.

Later that same day, I recorded in my journal:

> *I did it! I did it! I got Alina through the Commission! And as soon as I have enough "identifying information" on Alexandra, I'll go back and get approval for her. I can't believe it! Hallelujah!*

By the end of the week I had obtained Commission approval for Alexandra and scheduled a 28 March court date for Alina's adoption. Although I was thrilled that we had finally made progress, I was saddened by the realization that I would not make it home by Easter. My first month in Romania had been quite an emotional roller coaster.

On Sunday, 24 March 1991, the first LDS baptisms were held in Romania. It was quite a spiritual experience to see three people baptized who would shortly be leading the branch in Bucharest. I felt humble to be there.

The morning of Alina's court date, I was so excited that I woke up at 3:15 a.m. We arrived at the courthouse about 9:30 with Alina's birth mother and grandmother but had to wait until after noon to be seen. We finally were taken to a small office where half a dozen people were waiting for us. I felt guilty of some terrible crime. No one smiled or looked the least bit approving. The prosecutors started firing questions at me through the interpreter. They asked how many children I had and what their ages were. I wanted to sink through the floor as I explained that I already had three children, ages three, two, and one. They also asked who took care of my children. When I answered that I did, they appeared somewhat impressed. The last question they asked me was if, during the education of our children, it was all right to beat them. I thought I had misunderstood and said somewhat incredulously, "To beat them? No!" That response at least elicited a few approving smiles. Later, when I received a translated copy of the court decision, I learned that, instead of them being against us for already having three children, the court was in favor of the adoption because I was "an experienced, caring mother." The adoption was granted. I was able to get the fifteen-day waiting period shortened to just five days by signing the necessary waivers. Then I would be allowed to take Alina from the orphanage.

Later that same week, it became apparent that adopting Alexandra, the Down's syndrome baby, was going to be difficult, if not impossible. Once Alina's adoption was complete, my agent became reluctant to continue working for me on Alexandra's adoption.

Easter Sunday, 30 March, was the most emotional day of my whole trip. At church that morning, I started crying and couldn't stop for two hours, I was so sad and frustrated. In my journal, I wrote the following:

> *I am bottoming out, folks. We were supposed to be home by now, but here we sit, with the prognosis getting grimmer every day. I am really starting to get depressed. I almost feel like I've been tortured too long, and I'm slowly collapsing. Tears are very, very close to the surface, and I'm starting to feel like it's all I can do to just hang on for one more hour. I keep trying to pray "Thy will be done," but I just have to go home this weekend!*

I expected a call from Greg later that day. When the call came in, I poured out my frustrations. He didn't know what to say and was the sadder than I had ever heard him. I told him that I felt strongly about Alexandra and wanted to adopt her, but I was starting to question whether we could really get her. Maybe it was not meant to be. Greg said he didn't know, but they were praying for us—me, Alexandra, and Alina.

I then spoke to my mother. I gave her a brief synopsis of the situation, and asked her what she thought. She said, "Holly, I know you are coming home with those two little girls. I know that as surely as I know your name." She continued to say that when she first heard about the two little girls, the Spirit had confirmed to her that they belonged in our family. She told me to have faith in my Heavenly Father. I asked her what I should say in court when asked my reasons for wanting to adopt Alexandra. She said I should bear my testimony that I knew God wanted me to have this child to love and to raise. Her words comforted me greatly and gave me new courage.

I also asked for and received a blessing that day from Brother Price. Through the blessing, I was told that everything I had been promised in earlier blessings would be fulfilled. I was assured that my desire to come and adopt children was noble, and that Heavenly Father knew that I had made many preparations and sacrifices to be here. Brother Price then told me that it was very clear that I would take home two children. He also promised that once I got home, the time spent in Romania would be as nothing.

The blessing gave me the strength to carry on, and I needed it, because the next trial started all too soon. A few hours later, my agent came to visit. He felt that I had less than a one percent chance of getting Alexandra, and that he could no longer help me. I was devastated, but fortunately, after two days he arranged for a colleague to replace him.

The one wonderful part of the week was having the thrill of bringing little Alina Marie Richardson home from the orphanage. The whole world seemed a better place. The next day, I recorded in my journal:

> *She is really a sweet little girl, and not long after I got her, it seemed like she'd always been mine. It was hard to imagine that she came from a little sixteen-year-old's body, and that she'd spent some fourteen months in an orphanage without anything like a mother's love. She's sure got it now! The instant I held her in the orphanage, after she was officially mine, I thought, "Oh, who would want a newborn when they could have this!" Of course, my grandmother would say, "Every old crow thinks hers is the blackest!"*

Alina came with many orphanage-type behaviors, including rocking, sucking her fingers, sucking on her tongue, and several other self-comforting rituals. I knew she would outgrow these behaviors fairly rapidly, which indeed she did for the most part. The most agonizing results of her life in the orphanage were the night terrors, which didn't really start until she got home.

She frequently woke up terrified and would not let us touch her, yet did not want us out of her sight. I knew she was remembering past abuse.

My new agent made a court date for 9 April for Alexandra's adoption. The day in court dawned gloomy and rainy, but that did not dampen my positive feelings. I felt calm and assured all day. I spent quite a while sitting in front of the courthouse with her parents. It was awkward with no translator. At 9:30 we were told that the secretary had decided not to come in that day. We'd have to come back the next day. I still felt good, and we did not give up. By 10:45 my new translator had convinced the secretary to come in. We were taken into a little office to wait with three other women. The court proceedings were simple. The only question I was asked was if "Richardson" was my last name. Then it was official. I was astonished that things were so easy. The only hard part about it was that Mariana, Alexandra's birth mother, burst into tears as she signed the papers. It was much harder to adopt a child from a loving mother than one who didn't seem to know much about being a mother. I have come to realize, however, that Daniella must surely have grieved at one time or another, as virtually all birth mothers do.

After our court appearance, Mariana invited me to her home for lunch. It was just the two of us for a little while. She didn't speak a word of English, and my Romanian was certainly less than adequate. She called her sister, who left work, and came over to translate. Her English was minimal, but we got by. Mariana kept crying, and I really didn't know what to say. She grieved for the loss of her daughter, as her subsequent letters have shown. Even today, it sometimes feels strange to know that Alexandra was meant to be our daughter, but had to be born thousands of miles away to someone to whom I know we will always be close.

After we ate, Mariana went through the baby clothes of her oldest daughter, (who was never told she had a sister, but who asks for one all the time). She gave me a good-sized pile of clothes to take home. I really didn't know how many I'd actually be able to use, but I knew it was something she needed to do for Alexandra.

On Thursday I went to the orphanage to pick up Alexandra. I dressed her, gave a Cabbage Patch doll to a physically handicapped girl who had also captured my heart, and took my daughter home to my apartment. All that remained to do was the simple formality of obtaining a visa for my daughters to come to America. Once again, complications awaited me.

The next day I went to the embassy to have the girls seen by the officials so I wouldn't have to bring them on the day of my visa appointment. I asked the duty officer if I was going to have trouble with Alexandra. She said that according to regulations, Alexandra was excludable for a visa to enter the United States. That was just a nice way of saying she would be denied a visa. I started to cry. I was informed that in order to get an exemption granted, they would have to send a psychological evaluation of Alexandra to the Center for Disease Control (CDC) in Atlanta, Georgia, where a psychologist would review the case and determine if the exemption should be granted. I was given another form to take back to the Policlinic to have the psychological evaluation done.

I was devastated. I had hoped to be home by the next Wednesday, 17 April, our five-year wedding anniversary. I had thought that surely, after seven and a half weeks away from home, I would be home for my anniversary. Now it was impossible.

I took a taxi back downtown to the phone palace to call Greg. I talked and cried for thirty minutes. Greg tried to be positive, reminding me that this was really the last hurdle I had to jump. He said my mother had spoken to the CDC, but learned the psychologist only came in every two weeks, and he had just been in the day before. She had heard that he occasionally did phone exemptions, and we were hoping he would do that for us.

That weekend was incredibly difficult for me. My journal entries began to sound increasingly panicky and were full of desperation and pleadings to get home. While writing I had missed Michael's first words and first steps, I threw myself on the couch sobbing and screaming, just begging the Lord to get me out of Romania. The mental pain was almost more than I could bear. I started to feel cynical about everything.

On our anniversary, I called Greg to tell him I loved him. I also got to talk to Aaron. "Mama," he said. "Mama, I love you. Mama, please come home." I cried again. After the phone call I started praying for peace and comfort, telling my Heavenly Father that I knew that he could work yet another miracle for me. I looked up miracles in the index of the Book of Mormon and found a very appropriate verse:

> *O then despise not, and wonder not, but hearken unto the words of the Lord, and ask the Father in the name of Jesus for what things soever ye shall stand in need. Doubt not, but be believing, and begin as in times of old, and come unto the Lord with all your heart, and work out your own salvation with fear and trembling before him.*
> (Mormon 9:27)

That day we had our visa appointments. I got Alina's visa with no problem and was able to fax Alexandra's information, including the psychological evaluation, to the CDC. My mother phoned the CDC and strongly encouraged them to expedite things to get me home. All I do could then was wait and pray for a miracle. I waited at the embassy the rest of the day for the miracle, but according to those in charge, the response from CDC did not come in. I went home in tears.

Later I learned that Alexandra's exemption had indeed been granted and faxed to the embassy that same day, but somehow it had gotten lost in some other papers. As a result, I had to wait until the following Monday, an additional three days, to get clearance to bring Alexandra home with Alina and me. We left Romania that very day.

The flight to America was the most fantastic twelve hour trip I've ever taken. We spent the night in New York and then sat around at the airport until our flight for Utah left at 4:00 p.m. How I wished it were a one-hour flight, instead of seven! It seemed so long.

After we landed, I blocked the aisle trying to get out. I had two carry-on bags that weighed about thirty-five pounds each, plus my two girls. The plane was at the end of a long concourse, and because of extra airport security measures during the Gulf War, my family had to watch me walk the entire way. When I got closer, Aaron broke loose and ran out to meet me. A few steps later, someone took Alina, and I was in Greg's arms, kissing, laughing, and crying. He picked up Alexandra, and said, "Oh, Holly, she's the right one." He loved Alina just as much, of course, and also knew that she was meant to be in our family. He is a wonderful man; not many men would enthusiastically greet five children in five years of marriage.

Aaron talked all the way home, even though it was almost midnight. Elizabeth was happy and smiled and cooed a lot, but unfortunately, Michael had forgotten me. He clung to his daddy's leg, looking at me as if to say, "Who are you?" It took almost a week before I felt he was starting to like me again.

Those of us who were blessed enough to be able to go to Romania to adopt were required to give more than we thought we had—physically, emotionally, and financially. I had frequently given up before when things got tough, but I now know that I have strength and determination far beyond what I had previously imagined. I know that my experience of being in Romania will always give me courage and assurance in hard times to come. Indeed, I know with a surety born of a trial by fire that "with God, nothing is impossible."

Landon and Alexis as they appeared on their passport photos.

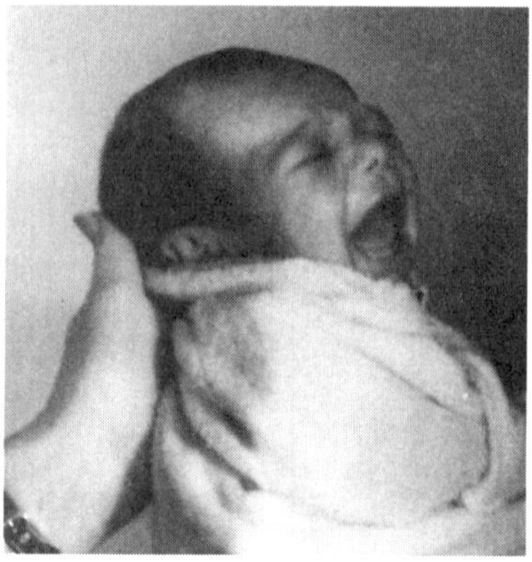

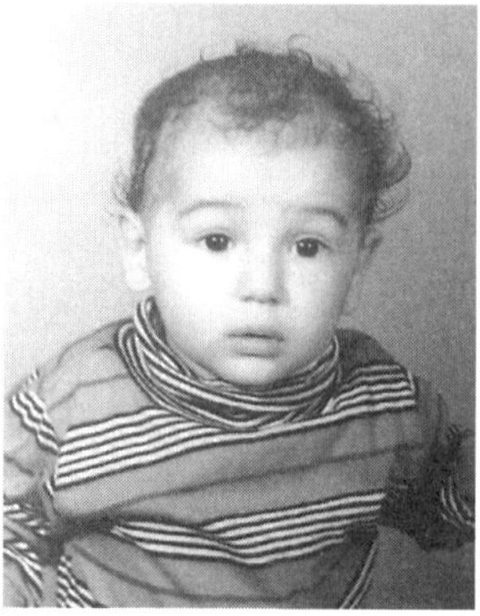

The Jensen Family

ALL IN THE LORD'S TIME

Kathy Chambers Jensen

Our story really started in April 1990 with a special segment of *20/20* that showed us the plight of the homeless and futureless Romanian children. My mind and heart were soon overcome by the grief and helplessness of these children. The report haunted me for several months, but the only thing I felt I could do was pray for these poor children, that some of their pain and emptiness would somehow be alleviated, and that they would find some happiness.

Several months later, a dear friend and neighbor called. I told her I was just heading out the door and expected her usual, "Oh, I'll let you go then." Instead I got an "Oh, well, uh—I really need to talk to you!"

"What's wrong?" I asked, a tinge of panic in my voice.

She finally burst out, all in one breath, "I'm going over to Romania to adopt some children. My husband and I have prayed about it, and we feel very strongly about our decision. We are asking a few people, whom we feel impressed to tell, and you are one of them. Do you want to go?"

The question finally opened up a barrier in my thinking. I desperately wanted to do this, but I also knew that I had to look at it very logically. My heart was willing, yet my mind was trying to be realistic.

Was there purpose in those strong feelings I'd had since seeing the show? Was I to be one of the "ways" or "means" that I had prayed for to help those orphaned children? Later that afternoon, when I had gotten my children down for their naps and the house was quiet and still, I knelt down and prayed earnestly to my Father. I asked him whether I should be directly involved with the adoptions taking place in Romania. In only a minute a warm, comforting feeling began to invade my body and soul. Doctrine and Covenants 9:8 reads:

> *But, behold, I say unto you, that you must study it out in your mind; then you must ask me if it be right, and if it is right I will cause that your bosom shall burn within you; therefore, you shall feel that it is right.*

I knew then that going to Romania was both the right and necessary thing to do.

Next came the task of explaining to my husband, Robert, what had transpired during the course of the day. It's difficult to work the subject of "Romania," let alone "adoption," into a casual dinner conversation. "By the way, dear, speaking of Romania…" Robert did not want to continue with this particular topic, and the subject fell flat. I could go no further without Robert's consent and help.

Through the grapevine, my friend and I heard about an upcoming meeting at the Salt Lake County Library. We were told that a few couples who had just gone through the Romanian adoption proceedings would be speaking. "Let's just go and listen," I said to Robert. "It can't hurt anything."

He reluctantly consented, but he let me know that he thought I was off my rocker. Robert was very defensive all the way to the library. "Why are we even going?" he asked. I couldn't understand how we could have such opposing views. The tension between us was unbelievable.

The room at the library was packed to capacity with over

200 people. "Well, Kathy," Robert commented, "I guess you are not the only crazy person around. You've got plenty of company." All during the meeting he kept craning his neck, looking around the crowded room, and saying louder than I would have liked, "Look at all these crazy people! Would you just look at them all!"

That night I prayed that, if it be right, Robert's heart would be softened. On Monday morning he said to me, "I guess you'd better get our home study scheduled if you are still determined to do this." I didn't even ask if he were serious. As soon as I got the kids off to school and Robert to work, I dashed to the phone to make an appointment.

Robert had softened a little, but he was not totally convinced. After the home study was completed, Robert told me his concerns. "We don't know whose problems or what problems we'd be bringing into our home. Will this really be fair to our children?" I had to admit, these were legitimate questions. They even made me question my own decision somewhat. Again, I went to our room that night in fervent prayer. Once again that warm, tingly sign of reassurance from the Holy Ghost dispelled my doubts.

Robert tried to be supportive, but he needed a stronger confirmation. I had completed mounds of paperwork that would soon be finalized. My friend had definitely decided she was going with or without me, and I knew I couldn't go without Robert's whole-hearted support. I began to fast and pray more fervently than I ever had before.

One night, Robert woke me up out of a sound sleep and said, "Kathy, I have been in turmoil for a very long time." My heart sank. I wasn't sure I wanted to hear what was coming next. He continued, "For this last little while, I have been fasting and praying and pleading with the Lord to help me know whether we should go to Romania and adopt. I want you to know, I finally have a peace inside of me, and I now know that this is the right thing to do." I knew how much he had struggled with the idea, how much turmoil and deep anxiety it had cost him, and how hard it had been for him to finally accept it. An overwhelming feeling of gratitude and complete joy filled my heart.

Robert made connections for me and my friend on a flight that would be leaving the following week. As fate would have it, our date of departure was 1 April, April Fool's Day. I should have taken this as a clue of just how our adventure would progress.

Maria, our agent, met us at the Bucharest airport. The next morning she took us to the Commission's Office, where we hoped obtain names of adoptable children. The Commission was a panel of women doctors who had a master list of all the available children in Romanian orphanages. The waiting room was crammed full of people from all over the world, Germany, Italy, France, England, and Canada—all with looks of anticipation on their faces.

Maria spoke to the receptionist for a very long time. After about thirty minutes, the receptionist waved us into the Commission president's office. As we walked into the room, the atmosphere felt stiff. The six women in the room were very businesslike. The president and another doctor were seated at the head of a large wooden desk, so large that it dwarfed the two small chairs in which we were to sit. While Maria spoke for us in Romanian, we sat directly facing the president. My friend and I felt very much like little children, not at all knowing what they were saying. Should we be stony faced, smile to show interest, or look forlorn in hopes that they would see how much we desired to adopt these children? Eventually we were given the names of two "normal" children, both located in an orphanage nearly four hours away.

We didn't realize it then, but we had just hurdled two major obstacles. First, no one was allowed into the Commission without an appointment, and appointments were being made over the phone for the following January. Second, the Commission was giving out names of handicapped children to all others that day.

We wasted no time getting to the orphanage. When we held these little children, our emotions took dips, curves, and turns. We tried not to get our hopes up, for we had yet to see their birth certificates. When I was handed the birth certificate of the child I was given, I was disappointed to see two parents listed. The American law stated that you could not adopt a child if there were a married mother and father. I was disheartened and discouraged to have to turn down this "nobody's child" because of legal formalities. I often wonder about that little girl and what happened to her. Is she still there, or did she have a chance with another person who was bound by fewer restrictions?

The little boy that my friend was given also had two parents on his birth certificate, but the mother had died, and the father had abandoned him at the time of her death. She was able to adopt him after a three-month ordeal.

I spent the following three weeks trying to locate a child that could be adopted, only to meet seven similar disappointments. I seemed to be running around in circles and felt the strong influence and stumbling blocks of the adversary in almost everything I did. When options started looking good and somewhat promising, another obstacle would fall in my path. Some were trivial, but others were major—I would be forced to give up the child I was working for and pray that there would be an opportunity to try again. Small obstacles it didn't make the heartache or disappointment any easier. The losses of these little children emotionally exhausted me.

Then, just as things looked like they couldn't get any worse, Maria, our Romanian agent, seemed to drop off the face of the earth. We could not contact her at her home or office. We were abandoned in a foreign country with no one to help us.

I remember the following Sunday at church after these horrible, frustrating, and fruitless three weeks. I felt completely discouraged and wondered what I was doing in Romania when I had a husband and four children who needed me and missed me as much as I missed them. It seemed like everyone around me was successful with their adoptions, but I had been denied similar success. Tears were near the surface, and I recall the song we sang in our English-speaking Gospel Doctrine class that morning: "Master, the Tempest is Raging." Tears welled up in my eyes as I sang the second verse.

> *Master, with anguish of spirit*
> *I bow in my grief today.*
> *The depths of my sad heart are troubled.*
> *Oh, waken and save, I pray!*
> *Torrents of sin and of anguish*
> *Sweep o'er my sinking soul,*
> *And I perish! I perish! dear Master.*
> *Oh, hasten and take control!*
> (*Hymns*, [Salt Lake City: The Church of Jesus Christ of Latter-day Saints, 1985], #105)

After returning home, I went to my room and prayed for forgiveness for my lack of faith and waning spirits and for God's continued protection and blessings on my loved ones back home. As I prayed, I felt impressed to write in my journal. This entry was the immediate answer to my prayer and gave me encouragement to continue on.

> *The purpose we have come here for, embedded in our mind,*
> *Our faith endures, and often tried, but mostly it is blind...*
> *But then one day in earnest prayer, a question I*

must ask,
The answer's clear, "Remain, my child; it's time
to do your task..."

That evening, as my roommate and I sat and visited, my dear friend from back home called. I told her what had happened with our Romanian agent, and she encouraged me to contact the agent she had used a few months ago when she was in Romania. I knew that this man was already working with fifteen other Americans and felt that he would not consider taking on two more people. Shortly after talking with her, my husband called and advised me to try this new avenue. Later, a friend from our little Romanian branch also called that evening and said that if we didn't have anyone else in particular we wanted to work with, she would talk to her agent to see if he would take on two more Americans. All three people, in the course of a few hours, gave me the name of the very same man. How much more obvious could my answer have been?

With no more hesitation on my part, I called him that night and asked if he would be able to help us. He told me that he was very busy; but when he learned our situation, he agreed to help us. It was the turning point we needed. That night, and many times later, I thought of this statement from Elder Neal A. Maxwell:

> *Therefore, how can you and I really expect to glide naively through life, as if to say, "Lord give me experience, but not grief, not sorrow, not pain, not opposition, not betrayal, and certainly not be forsaken. Keep from me, Lord, all those experiences which made Thee what Thou art! Then, let me come and dwell with Thee and fully share thy joy!"* ("Lest Ye Be Wearied and Faint in Your Minds," *Ensign* [May 1991]: 88)

A few days later we were literally on the road to adopting children. Our agent arranged a driver who took us to a village out in the country. We found a little boy there who for safety purposes needed to be taken out of his surroundings that day. My friend and I both knew that this child was to be hers. I had no feelings of jealousy over this decision. Each night I ended the day with hope in my heart, tears in my eyes, and a prayer on my lips. Although I still had not found my child, I wrote in my journal what we, as mothers, felt in Romania as we pursued adopting our children.

My tiny one, I look at you and wonder how I came,
To be so very fortunate, and blessed to call your name.
To add you to our family, where love and dreams abound,
Your spirit and the joy you bring, there's much more to be found.
You're like a tiny blossom, still wet with morning dew,
With nurturing and promises of things I'll show to you.
For now, I'll keep you safe and warm, for you are still so small,
But one day soon, as you prepare, your destiny may fall
Back to your roots, where you were born, to fulfill your mission call.

As time went on, we found ourselves in a kind of family situation with many other Americans trying to adopt, many of whom were attending church in a very small Romanian branch. Because we were all feeling anxious and frustrated, branch. Because we were all feeling anxious and frustrated, we began to bond with one another. Rules and laws were changing continually. Paperwork we had come over with was no longer sufficient, and more clearances and detailed information were required. In order to keep our sanity and to keep each other informed on the most up-to-date information, my roommate and I decided to have a get-together every Sunday at 6 p.m. at our apartment. We would swap war stories and laugh and visit. It was therapeutic for us to laugh and talk because we were all so close to tears. One night, as we faced our third month in Romania, one question seemed to be on everyone's mind: "Would you have done it, if you had known then what you know now?" I couldn't get the question out of my mind. Once again I wrote in my journal that I would have undoubtedly come to Romania even if I had been completely aware of the trials that awaited me.

Finally, with the help of our new Romanian friends, I found a beautiful fourteen-month-old little boy available for me to adopt. I couldn't believe it. My turn had finally come, but timing was critical. Rumors flew that if you didn't have a court date in the books, you were out of luck. Since it had not yet been determined whether my court date would be acknowledged or not, I was frightened and discouraged. After all this time, effort and hard work, how could this possibly be happening? In my journal I articulated my concerns and my resolve to continue with the adoption:

> *The doors are closing, little ones; the time is getting near.*
> *The adversary knows our cause, there's much for him to fear.*
> *So we must not be swayed by him, whose thoughts are to deceive.*

A greater strength, if we but ask, we'll
readily receive.
The righteous shall be justified. Take heed in
all you do
Remember souls are precious here, preparing
lives anew.

The court date for my little boy, who by now was sixteen months old, finally arrived. I waited outside the courthouse until late afternoon, when the prosecutor suddenly stormed out the front door and down the street in a rage. My agent and his workers ran after her, but she would not reason with them. They ran back to the courtroom and learned that she and the judge had gotten into a heated argument and had cancelled the remaining appointments for the day.

While waiting a full week for my rescheduled court date, my agent and I returned to the little town to finish some trivial paperwork. During the course of the day my agent heard of another child available for adoption. He asked if I was interested in seeing the child. Although my track record for proceeding with the adoption had not been encouraging, I said yes. I was shown the teeniest baby girl I had ever seen. A warm, tingling sensation filled my entire being as I laid my eyes on her. Though I only saw her for a few seconds I agreed to adopt her. Later, her unwed mother consented for me to proceed. Had it not been for the delay in court proceedings the previous week, I would not have been in that little town on that particular day to choose this child for my own. All occurred in the Lord's time.

My final chance for a court date was nearing its arrival. The remaining days were filled with endless inner turmoil and continual anxiety. My husband called me with hopes of hearing words of encouraging details, but I had been told not to be too explicit on the phone about dates, times, or places

Robert was quite baffled by the end of our brief and uninformative conversation.

I had many sleepless nights; one night in particular, after lying in bed for hours in restless fits, I wondered if this would all work out. Had I come all the way to Romania in vain, or was I here to learn a valuable lesson? I almost resented the night coming; I had so much unfinished work left to do before my court date, and each document I needed took so long to obtain. Although I was close to completing the adoptions, I felt that if I didn't hurry and get things done, everything would close up on me. I got out of bed and started writing down my thoughts. After reading what I had felt impressed to write, I knew that it was my answer, my relief poem, that assured me I had done all that I could possibly do. If it was meant to work out, it would; if not, then I had learned many other important lessons along the way.

A comfort came to me last night—or was it early morn?
My thoughts entangled in my dreams, and I was truly torn.
What should I do? What will affect my future I'll decide.
My heart was torn, my thoughts were mixed, as I laid there and cried.
In quiet darkness came these thoughts: "Why useless worries ponder?
It's in my hands, no longer yours. There's no more need to wonder.
You've done all you were sent to do. The rest is left for me.
Soon hearts will soften, minds will quicken—just you wait and see."
So in my solace, words I gave of thanks for

So in my solace, words I gave of thanks for
comfort given,
I am not here in vain, I know. This plan was
Heaven given.

As I went to court at the end of the week, the "plan," given to so many of us who went over to Romania, had finally proven fruitful. I was given two beautiful children. Sixteen-month-old Landon weighed a mere 16 pounds and didn't know how to crawl or walk. He had never been fed anything more than two bottles a day in his life. When given anything solid or of any consistency, he would gag or vomit because he hadn't been shown how to chew. He didn't know how to play with toys; they were as foreign to him as food.

I also received the tiniest of babies, a little girl whom we named Alexis. At birth she had weighed six pounds, but by now she was a mere three pounds. Just before the court hearing, my Romanian agent told me that her doctors had told him that she was probably suffering from hydroencephala (water on the brain) because her head was so much larger than her body. Later I found out that her head looked so much bigger because her body was shrinking. Her soft spots were all sunken, and her head was misshapen. I was told that she could have serious medical problems if I took her home with me, but I knew that this little girl needed the chance to survive. If left in Romania, she would die. She was malnourished, dehydrated, and starving to death.

When I took Alexis to my Bucharest apartment, I undressed her for her first bath. I was not prepared for the sight I saw. This baby was nothing but bones and loose, saggy skin hanging from her tiny limbs. Her legs and arms were no bigger around than my little finger. She wore no diaper. The rags I unwrapped were filled with urine and feces, which she had been lying in for an extensive period of time. Her skin was red and scalded from the waist down. As I tried to gently wash away the waste that had hardened onto her little bony behind, I had to stop; her skin was so raw that it was actually tearing away from her bones.

Thankfully, that's all behind us now. These same beautiful little children are now thriving, not only on food, but also on love. They are walking, running, and even talking. One of the most beautiful sounds to come from their tiny lips is the word, "Mama!"

I often think of those brave mothers who consented to their children's adoptions in hopes that the children would have a better life, a better existence, and, in the case of my daughter, a chance to survive. I hope they know of the love we have for these little ones, and that we cherish them as one of our most valuable possessions. As I look back at the events that took place in Romania I am vividly aware that each event took place only at the proper time. I am thankful for the Lord's intervention. I am also aware that events occurred in the Lord's timeframe, not mine.

Caitlin LaVange

A DIFFERENT KIND OF SWEETHEART

Don and Dorise LaVange

On Valentine's Day my husband, Don, and I celebrate both our love for each other and for a special little girl who is now part of our family. Just one year ago, we discovered the possibility of adopting Romanian children. We were at a gathering of Young Women leaders, taking a break from the usual meetings and enjoying Valentine's Day with our husbands. One of the women, DeAnna Ball, mentioned that she was going to adopt two children from Romania. Her husband, Terry, would spend two months in Hungary that summer and cross the border to Romania to adopt the children. Two days later we called them and asked if we could go with Terry. Our motivations for going were purely selfish—we wanted another baby. We hadn't seen the *20/20* shows and knew little of the orphans in Romania.

We already had three girls; our youngest was five years old. At the time of her birth, we felt certain another baby would join our family; but to our frustration, five years passed by fruitlessly. During that time we visited a fertility specialist. Although basic tests revealed nothing abnormal, I was still unable to conceive. Eventually I decided it was silly to continue going to the fertility specialist when I already had three beautiful children. However, every month brought new tears as we realized once again that I wasn't pregnant. I tried to comfort myself with the thought that it just wasn't meant to be; I should just forget it. But I couldn't resolve the strong feeling that another child awaited us.

Don: After five years Dorise began a new crusade. Adoption! She talked about it until I felt like I was drowning. I thought I could never love another person's child. Too much of the inherent love must be tied up in the delivery room or in the genetics of it all.

In December 1989, a friend called me from Idaho and asked if we were interested in adopting a baby. She knew of a girl that was due in a couple of weeks and needed someone to adopt her child. I would have jumped at the chance to adopt this baby, but my husband was not prepared; adoption terrified him. Could he ever love someone else's baby like his own?

Don: I wanted to do this for my wife, but inwardly I dreaded it. Someone else's baby! What if it were ugly? What if it were dull-witted? Some might say that one takes his chances even with naturally born children, but I was pretty convinced that those things couldn't happen to us. Eventually I attempted to live with the idea. I could be nice to the child. I didn't have to be in love with it. But then I got cold feet. Despite how much Dorise wanted a baby, my genetic chauvinism had gotten the best of me, and I told the contact no. I knew Dorise felt that we had let a golden opportunity slip by, but I simply felt we had avoided a nightmare.

We passed on that opportunity. However, the Lord prepared us to pursue adoption when the time was right. Don had several key experiences in the following year that resolved his adoption concerns. He spoke with several people who had been adopted as children. He visited a family in California who had adopted eight children and saw how the children enriched that family. An especially memorable experience occurred when a close friend told Don that they were told in the temple that their adopted children literally became their children when they were sealed together as a family.

The Lord was preparing Don during this time, but neither one of us realized it until one week after I proceeded with some of the work that related to the Romanian adoption. Don was still struggling to support to my efforts fully.

Don: I couldn't think of a good reason not to. It seemed sort of romantic and adventurous, and I sat back for the next few weeks while Dorise made phone calls and filled out paperwork. I paid only partial attention. I'm not sure I really believed that something this wild would ever come off. But before I knew it, we were at commitment time; it was all happening so fast. I began to get emotionally involved. Each evening Dorise would tell me what she had done and would tell me more about the Romanian orphans. My heart was touched. Maybe I could be a real humanitarian, and it would mean so much to Dorise.

One day I was overwhelmed with all of the events that had happened in Don's life over the last year which had affected his feelings about adoption. As we talked about these experiences, he also realized that this seemed to be something we had been prepared to do. We both felt the Lord would support us in it.

This was in March 1991. We planned to go to Romania in August with DeAnna and her husband, but we felt an urgency to complete the paperwork as soon as possible. I spent many hours on the phone getting names, stories, and suggestions. Then in early April, the news came that Romanian adoptions would be suspended as of 1 May. If we were to complete this task we would have to go soon. We realized that because of the timing, DeAnna and I would have to go without our husbands. Just the week before, we had completed our home studies, collected copies of the documents that were needed in the Romanian courts, and turned in all of our paperwork to United States Immigration and Naturalization Services (INS).

The next key to our success was to find a good Romanian agent to help us. Although DeAnna and I both talked with everyone we could think of to get recommendations for a good agent, we were not successful. On an amazing Saturday, DeAnna was able to get a phone call through to a man in Romania who said, "Yes I will help you. Come in ten days."

On Sunday I found myself asking Heavenly Father, "Is this what I should be doing? Please tell me." I felt a warm answer: "Look back on the things that have happened in your life since February. Haven't I given you the answer already?"

We spent the next week preparing for the trip. The first task was buying airplane tickets, but the bulk of the money that we had planned to use wouldn't be available to us for several more weeks. We tried all avenues with no success. I remember well my husband's phone call telling me that we couldn't gather the funds we needed in time. I would just have to call DeAnna and tell her I couldn't go. I hung up the phone and cried, wondering why so many things had happened up to this point to get us where we were.

Don: I called all the places that were always telling me I could get an unsecured loan, but they laughed at me when I told them I needed $7,000. They had meant that I could borrow $300. What did I have to secure such a loan? I called Dorise and said that I didn't know where to get the money; she should tell DeAnna to go without her. I could hear the pain in her quiet response. As I hung up I thought that it was really all for the best anyway and even felt relieved. Afterwards, though, I felt like I could not look Dorise in the face without making one more effort. I called someone I knew had the resources and basically begged for a loan. To my amazement, after hearing what it would be used for, he agreed to lend me the money. I called Dorise back and told her she could go. Scarcely thirty minutes had gone by since I had told her no.

The next few days we gathered food and all other possible items that DeAnna and I might need for an eight-week stay. We figured our clearance from INS would be what would detain us for eight weeks in Romania. The night before we were to fly a television show aired which negatively portrayed the Romanian adoptions. We had no idea the impact that publicity would have on our ability to bring our adopted children home. The next morning, 15 April, our plane left.

We left New York on Tarom, the Romanian airline, and what seemed like days later we arrived in Bucharest. I'll never forget the feeling of looking around me at that foreign place and knowing that I didn't have the power to do anything about my situation. DeAnna and I were completely in the hands of someone greater, and those hands carried me for about two weeks. I felt comforted as if I was being cradled, guided, and cared for. Every day I became aware of a different hurdle to overcome, and I prayed with all my heart for the help I needed to make this adoption happen.

We arrived in Romania on Tuesday evening and met with our agent to discuss the adoption requirements. Wednesday morning our driver and translator helped us make the first phone calls to our waiting husbands.

Don: I had not been in the habit of praying, but I began to gather my children around me to pray often. I was very worried about Dorise. I didn't hear from her for a day and a half. Finally, in the middle of the night I heard the phone ring, and I struggled to wake up. I heard the foreign voice of a Romanian operator who put Dorise on the line. I could barely hear her voice because of all the static. At times the connection broke, leaving sentences unfinished. She seemed so far away, and I felt like I was talking to someone on the other side of the veil.

Don felt strongly that I should look for a baby girl, but girls, especially newborns, were not easy to find. Still, I had the most comforting feeling that the Lord was watching over me and that the right things would happen. On Wednesday DeAnna found two boys at a hospital two hours outside of Bucharest. On Friday we returned to this hospital because we had heard there was a baby girl there that could be adopted. We were taken down long, dark hallways, up to the floor where the children were. A very sweet doctor led us into a room lined with cribs. Each crib held two or three babies. One week-and-a-half-old girl was taken out of her crib for me to see. At the time I didn't have any overwhelming feelings about this particular child. I did know that I wanted a newborn baby girl, things had fallen into place to get us there, and we didn't have much time ahead of us. I agreed to her adoption immediately; the confirmation of this decision came later.

Don: Dorise always had a feeling that I would be the one to recognize our daughter, and I had the same thought as well. I was very worried, because now it seemed that Dorise had that responsibility. I called her each day to ask if she found a baby yet. Finally one day she said yes, but she cautioned me that she had no special feeling about this baby, and there was no guarantee that we could complete the adoption. But for me, it had happened. I was overwhelmed with recognition for this girl. I wept openly on the phone and told Dorise that I knew that this was our daughter. I have never doubted it since.

Since we had so many papers to gather for the adoption, we were near the hospital nearly every day, and of course DeAnna and I wanted to see our children. A few days later our driver, Christina, took us back to hold the babies for a few minutes. As I took that little girl in my arms and looked down at her face, I was surprised to see the face of one of my own children. It seemed so impossible that I looked away and back again to see if this baby still resembled my child. She did—this baby looked like one of my babies. Overcome, I kept looking away and back again.

I wanted to spend all day with her, but our time was short, and soon we were on the road again. After several minutes of silence I turned to DeAnna and said, "The weirdest thing happened." I told her how that sweet little baby had suddenly looked like one of my babies. DeAnna had seen it too. There had been a change in the baby's face. Many times in the days to come, I reflected back on that experience for comfort and solace; I still had many problems to be overcome, and time was running out.

My court date was postponed three times. It hurt more each week as I thought of my baby lying in the hospital. Her eyes were beginning to cross because she had nothing on which to focus. By the time our court date arrived, we heard of more struggles ahead. Many people were completing adoptions and were then being denied visas to take their children home. I might also find myself in that situation if I completed this adoption. Again we put all our faith and trust in the Lord. We had seen his hand in so many situations that we couldn't deny his assistance. With that faith, I completed the adoption and brought my daughter home to our small apartment.

As I unwrapped her, I noticed blisters up and down the insides of her arms and legs and on her little hands. She was a very strong baby, and all of her squirming in the tightly swaddled wrappings had left her delicate skin blistered. The thought of her lying in that crib screaming for five weeks made my heart ache. With powder, lotion, and air, she healed within a few days, and I thought, "No one will ever believe she was so blistered."

As I spent the next two weeks gathering the paperwork needed to obtain a visa for my baby, I found great comfort in the scriptures. As tired as I was at night, and even though I knew how early the baby would be waking up in the morning, I felt I must read at least a little bit. I remember reading in Alma about faith the size of a small seed, and how it can sprout and begin to grow. This and other scriptures about having faith and trusting in the Lord seemed to speak directly to me. It amazed me that every night I found new comfort in the scriptures.

Daily we received news of friends who were denied visas. DeAnna and I felt that of the three babies we had between us, it was very possible that only one could receive a visa. Don was busy at home preparing documents in case our visa was denied. Though emotionally spent, somehow he kept strong.

At last my papers were in order, and I had an appointment on Thursday. I began fasting, because that was the only way I felt I could show my faith. I had to prepare myself for a denial, but I remembered the strength in my husband's voice as he told me that I needed once again to have faith; if we were meant to receive the visa, we would. He strongly felt that I would come home soon. Our children were almost out of school and had nowhere to go during the day. My five-year-old had been moved around from person to person for almost two months now and was beginning to suffer emotionally, and my ten-year-old was crying herself to sleep at night.

On Thursday I went to the embassy with many other Americans. I was called to a window and told that my daughter had a visa. I could come back that afternoon and pick up the completed paperwork. For me, it was a miracle; but as we had feared, DeAnna's two babies were among those whose visas were denied. She would have to remain in Romania.

When I returned to my apartment I was so elated that I called Don, even though it was 3:00 a.m. in the United States. "We are coming home!" I exclaimed through my tears. We left the next morning, seven weeks from my arrival in Romania. We spent one wonderful night in New York—we weren't home yet, but we were in the United States of America!

On Saturday night our plane was scheduled to arrive at 8:00 p.m., but it arrived about 30 minutes early. I held my baby, my treasure, closely as I walked to the baggage claim area. Somehow she seemed even more mine now that I had landed in Salt Lake. As I watched and waited, I saw my husband and three special little girls burst through the airport doors. They came running with open arms to claim their new sister. They had prayed for this moment almost as long and hard as I had. Because they too wanted that baby, they were able to bear all that they had to bear to get her. She had been a fussy baby and at first hadn't found any comfort in my arms. I worried how she would respond now with more unfamiliar arms reaching out to hold her. As we got to the car and I handed her to her new sisters, they looked into her eyes and talked to her. She looked into their eyes and smiled and loved them.

Don: The morning of the day my wife would come home, I received a letter from her which contained a picture of the little girl who was my new daughter. I think I showed the whole world that photo. When I spotted my wife in the airport, I ran to her. I first hugged her and felt so relieved to have her home. Then I took my daughter into my arms. I saw her eyes, and her smile and fell remarkably and incredibly in love. I am convinced that our Father in Heaven heard my prayers, my wife's prayers, and my daughters' prayers, and gave us this specific child in answer to our hearts' desires. I don't know when such things are decided, nor do I care. I know that she was chosen to be ours. I believe that if we hadn't listened, if we hadn't sacrificed, and if we hadn't been willing to follow his voice, she would have been given to another and blessed someone else's life.

Now, almost a year later, we look at our newest little sweetheart and realize that sometimes windows of opportunity are opened to us. If we are prepared and willing our lives may be blessed more than we could ever possibly imagine. The Lord is aware of our needs, desires, and situations. He answers prayers, and, yes, miracles do happen.

Don: I tell everyone about her. I tell them she's from Romania and that she's adopted. Sometimes I sort of hold her up in public so people will ask. I love to tell them about the babies there, how my wife was so brave, and how lucky we were to get this one. Inevitably, someone shakes his head and says how wonderful we must be to be willing to adopt.I shake my head back and try to tell them that for us, there was no unselfishness. Our daughter was born there, we had to go and get her. I would travel to the ends of the earth to get any of my babies. Wouldn't anyone?

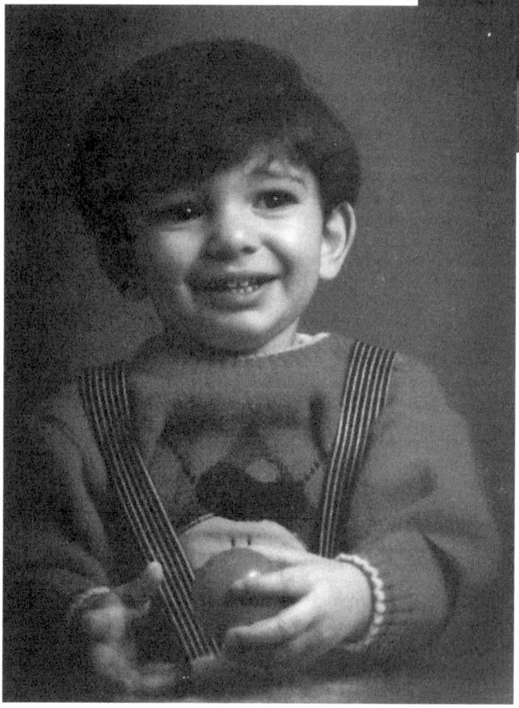

Cody and Alex Ball

TWO BOYS CLOSE IN AGE

DeAnna Ball

"I hope you believe in prayer," the pediatrician told me as I recovered in the hospital bed after giving birth to my fourth child, Dan, who was born with several life-threatening complications. "I have done all I can do for him," she said. "Now it is up to God."

My husband Terry and I daily called upon the power of prayer and the power of the priesthood to offer the blessings of health that Dan needed. Within weeks he was perfectly healthy. One doctor, an elder in our stake, told me that it was the power of the priesthood that had made Dan's recovery possible more than anything the physicians had done.

As I cared for Dan during the following months, I had a strong feeling that I should have two boys together, very close in age. However, I didn't become pregnant again for several years, and halfway through the pregnancy I miscarried the baby. More years passed, and other pregnancies also ended in miscarriage. We felt sure that I could never carry another baby full term. Where were the two boys close in age that I had felt so strongly about?

As I grieved over my losses, a friend suggested I consider adoption. There was a familiar truth in what she said, as if I were rediscovering something I had inwardly already known. I did not have any idea how to make it become a reality, but I decided to watch for adoption opportunities.

During the April 1990 general conference, Elder Thomas S. Monson gave news of the Church's growth in countries that had recently overthrown communism. He also told about the thousands of orphans in Romania and described their terrible plight. The Church had arranged to provide humanitarian missionaries, vaccines, medical dressings, and other urgently needed supplies for the orphanages.

Almost instantly, I knew that one of those babies was mine and I became preoccupied with the thought of adopting a Romanian orphan. I knew that if I didn't do all that I could to pursue my feelings, the wondering would haunt me for the rest of my life.

My husband, Terry, thought it preposterous to adopt a Romanian orphan. He was in the second year of an intense doctoral study program and supporting our family on a part-time salary. He really did not want to talk about it, but suggested that if I still felt the same after he graduated, we could talk about it then.

I didn't talk about adopting in Romania anymore, but I could not get the idea out of my mind. One day the feelings were especially strong, and I poured out my heart in prayer to God, asking what I should do. My answer came quickly and directly. I did not hear any words with my ears, but the confirmation came straight to my soul—I would adopt in Romania. Strangely, though, I was instructed not to bother Terry about it. God would prepare the way for me, and I should wait and watch for that day.

Nine months later, on a cold January evening, Terry came home excited with news that his lifelong friend Glen and his wife Tara were going to Romania to adopt a baby. The same sense of urgency filled my being that I had felt nine months before. "Oh," I exclaimed, "we should go with them!"

I could hardly believe it when Terry responded, "Wouldn't that be great?" My heart began to race. It was the moment I had been waiting for. God had prepared the way for me. We both were excited this time and began immediately to figure out how and when we could get to Romania.

Terry had to work that evening, and while he was gone I told our four children that I thought we would soon be adopting in Romania. Their eyes got big, and they wanted to know how many babies we would adopt. I felt impressed to say we would adopt two children.

I worried about how I would tell Terry my new idea of adopting two children, but I fell asleep before he came home. That night he dreamed he was a basketball star playing in a big tournament in Europe. To his surprise, when he looked up to see the spectators the stands were full of cribs. Every crib had two babies in it, and they were all looking at him. When morning came he told me about his dream. "You will think this is strange," he said, "but I want to adopt two babies." The Spirit had led both of us independent of one another to the same conclusion.

Terry had also been figuring out how to get to Romania. He had been invited by other scientists to spend July and August in Hungary that summer doing the archaeological research needed for his doctorate. He decided to accept the invitation. Since Hungary was next to Romania, he could adopt the babies before returning home. We immediately began the long process of completing the pre-adoption requirements for United States immigration officials.

A couple in our neighborhood, Don and Dorise LaVange, decided to come with us to Romania. Glen and Tara, however began to have doubts and decided not to go. As it turned out, their long-awaited local adoption finally came through. They had been the answer to my prayers, and now their prayers had been answered.

Early one April morning I woke up with an overwhelming impression to telephone several people who had adopted in

Romania. One of those I called, Ginger Larsen, told me the news reports claimed that on 1 May all adoptions there would be suspended. Unless we left immediately, it would be too late.

Terry was in the middle of the university semester and would not be free until June. Dorise's husband couldn't leave his work either. She and I realized the two of us would have to make the perilous journey without our husbands. That's when I began to understand why Heavenly Father had let me know a year in advance that I would be adopting in Romania. If I hadn't known for sure it was the right thing to do, I would have been too frightened to go.

After finding a Romanian agent, next problem was that I didn't even have money for airline tickets, let alone all the other expenses. My sister told me to go to my credit union. On the application I wrote down the amount a friend had told me the trip would cost. Then, thinking that somehow I could get by, I crossed it out and wrote an amount several thousand dollars less. When I explained to the loan officer why I needed the money, she became very quiet and left the room for a few minutes. When she returned, she said that the loan had been approved, but for the larger amount that I had crossed out. She said she could read it under my scratch marks and felt sure I would need it. As it turned out, my stay in Romania was so long and costly that I needed every penny of that money.

When we arrived in Bucharest, I realized that I had made a big mistake by putting a large part of my money into traveler's checks. I was told they were absolutely useless in Romania because there was no place to cash them. I almost panicked, but on our first visit to the United States Embassy, I sat next to a military man who had just adopted a baby girl. During the conversation, he turned to me and said that he was going to the Bank of International Exchange to cash his travelers checks. I was amazed; I had mentioned nothing of my problem to him. We visited the bank the next day and learned that it was the only place in Romania where they could be cashed. This occurrence witnessed to me that God was by my side, leading me each step of the way.

Our agent had arranged an apartment for Dorise and me to stay in. By Romanian standards it was wonderful, but one window didn't close and the heater rarely worked, so it was usually very cold. There weren't any bedrooms, but two couches were available for us to sleep on.

John was our translator, and Christina, who spoke no English, was our driver. After about four days Christina began to speak English quite fluently. "Never before did I speak English until you came!" she told us. I had been praying for the gift of tongues as I studied the Romanian language each night, and the Lord blessed me to understand many things, but the greatest surprise was that he blessed Christina to speak English. Numerous times she had to explain to John what we were saying.

On our second day in Romania, we traveled a small dusty road for two hours to a hospital that contained a pediatric unit which housed abandoned babies. After waiting for permission to enter, we followed Christina in. The hospital was so dark inside that patients, seeking a bit of light, crowded the hallway near the door, and we had to make our way through a mass of bodies. We went down several long, cold hallways, up two flights of stairs, and waited on a wooden bench until we were invited by a kindly doctor to enter her office.

We were seated on a threadbare couch, and I was told that there was a baby boy for me to see. By now I was shaking inside and out. Our time and opportunities were very limited. I knew I would have to make a decision on the child as we sat there. Soon a nurse carried in a baby boy, upset and crying terribly. His head was covered by two or three caps, but I could see several wisps of his blonde hair. His large, blue eyes were filled with fright and misery. His face was covered with a red rash, and I could only imagine the condition of his skin under his wet, gray rags. I was told that he was abandoned because of chronic illnesses. He was currently suffering from a bronchitis that had lasted several months, but the doctor assured me he would soon be well.

I felt immediate compassion for the baby and tried to comfort him. His rags were so soaked with urine that my clothes and arms also became damp. To my delight, he responded to my attention and stopped crying as he reached out to pull my red hair. We all laughed, but when I held him by the trunk to let his feet touch a nearby table, he screamed with pain. His legs had atrophied from disuse.

I wasn't sure that he was my child, but I had a feeling that if I offended the doctor, she would not help us anymore. I am sure she would have said, "I have no other children available for adoption." As I thought about what to say, John told me that the baby had been born in April 1990. I remembered that it was April 1990 when I had received my first impression to go to Romania and wondered if this was the baby I had felt was waiting for me. Although I didn't feel an instant bonding, I knew that I could grow to love him as my own and decided to name him Austin.

A nurse took Austin away, and Christina told the doctor that I wanted two babies. She was surprised. To the Romanians, it is difficult to provide enough food for even one child. With some persuasion, the doctor opened her files. She spoke in Romanian, but I was able to understand some of the words, and my heart leaped when I heard her mention a two-week-old baby boy. When I saw the baby, I marveled at his beauty. All I could see was his face, but it was enough to win my heart. His lashes were wonderfully long and his face fresh and new. I knew I couldn't leave Romania without him. I would name him Cody.

A few days later Dorise was shown a little girl in the same hospital. She had been there all along, but another American couple had been considering adopting her. They had decided on a different baby, but worried constantly about the girl until, quite by coincidence, they found out that Dorise had decided to adopt her.

We were busy from morning till evening over the next two weeks trying to gather all the necessary papers for our court date. To our dismay, however, week after week the home studies for these children's birth mothers were delayed. The only man who could do them was always too busy. Dorise and I were worried about the babies having to stay so long in the hospital. It gave me a dark, haunting feeling to hear those newborn cries and have to walk away, knowing nobody would respond.

One of the papers we needed for court was a health certificate for the babies. I had felt strongly to ask for blood tests, but John kept telling me that it had been done, and I would see it on the health certificate. We finally got the certificate, but it made no mention of blood tests. It took a good deal of persuasion, but John finally asked the doctor for blood samples from the babies. I got a sick feeling when the results came back; Austin was sick with much more than bronchitis—he was dying of AIDS. He would not be allowed to enter the United States. I could not adopt him. A horrible nightmare had come true.

The doctor did not believe the test result. "You must still adopt him," she told me. Even John angrily chastised me, but I had no choice. I would have a child that I could never bring home. The doctor insisted that the test be repeated and sent two nurses and us to his room to take the blood.

I had come to love Austin and did not think I could bear to see him again, knowing that I would be leaving him for good. But the doctor had ordered us to watch the blood being drawn so that we could be sure it was his blood being tested. Two young nurses brought in a cardboard box containing a few supplies. They found a needle to pierce a vein, but baby veins are very tiny, and although the nurse probed viciously, she could not draw blood. Austin screamed with pain as she continued to poke and prod. I knelt by his side to hold him through his ordeal. The screaming continued for a full minute, then two, three—even four minutes passed. Could this go on forever? I broke down in tears. At last I could stand no more, and from the depth of my soul pleaded out to God through silent prayer, "Oh God, help this little soul!"

Immediately the blood began to flow, and both the nurses' hands were stained bright red as they tried to position a vial to catch the spilling blood. The vial filled quickly, and they began wiping the spilt blood with rags. Then they hurried to wash their red hands, and in horror I realized that if they had the tiniest cut on their hands, they could now be infected with the deadly virus.

The second test showed identical results. Austin was taken to a hospital for very sick babies, and I never saw him again. I felt the same pain that I had felt years before after each miscarried pregnancy.

It was a horrible time to be alone, halfway across the world from Terry. I wanted him with me to comfort me and to help make the next decision that faced me. If I started on a new adoption, I had no guarantee that it would be honored by the courts, since the following day was 1 May. Even if it were honored, I didn't think I had the strength to stay in Romania any longer than it would take to finish Cody's adoption, which was already taking a full four weeks. I wanted to be home. I almost wished I had never come. Where could I go to find the peace that I needed?

When we arrived back at our apartment, I remembered a hill in a beautiful park in downtown Bucharest where Elder Russell M. Nelson had given the dedicatory prayer to bring the gospel to Romania. I thought that if an apostle of the Lord Jesus Christ had been there to offer the dedicatory prayer, maybe I could find a spirit of peace there to calm my troubled heart; I asked Dorise to go with me.

We began walking on a crowded street we had never been on before. Shortly after passing the Lebanon Airline office, an old man walked right up to my face and spat. I instinctively screamed, but quickly covered my mouth and somehow kept walking without missing a pace. How could anyone hate me so much? I felt terrified and wondered if it was foolish for me, an American, to be out on the street so soon after the Gulf War.

At last we reached the park where we found the little hill from which a stream of water breaks forth. It was a public place, so I could not kneel to pray, but in my heart I poured out my troubles to God. I prayed for Austin, for Cody, and for my children at home. I prayed for help to heal quickly from the wounds in my heart so that I could go on. I felt far away from home and began to doubt my faith. If I could only know for sure that God could still hear my prayers and answer me.

It was getting late, and we had to leave before the darkness settled in. As we left the hillside, I was frightened by footsteps running up right behind me. I turned to see a beautiful Romanian girl in her early twenties. She saw the frightened look on my face and apologized for startling me. Then she handed me a folded note and in perfect English said, "Someone asked me to give this to you." Then she kissed my cheek and turned and ran away as quickly as she had come. The note simply said, "You are too beautiful to be so sad." A little heart was sketched under the message. I walked home with renewed comfort, knowing that my prayer had been heard. In a city with so much suffering, the thought that anyone would care to cheer me, a stranger, with such a touching message warms my heart to this day.

That night I called Terry and asked if I should just adopt Cody or stay to find a brother for him. I was desperately hoping he would let me adopt Cody and come home, but he was very firm. Even if it took several more weeks, we needed to find Cody a Romanian brother.

After speaking to Terry, I called several American women who I knew had been searching for babies in Romania and asked what babies they had found but not pursued. I wrote down the details of about four or five babies, but one of them made my heart leap with hope. There was a nine-day-old baby boy who had been abandoned by his impoverished, unmarried mother. Even without seeing him, I knew that I wanted him and would stay for as long as it took to get him.

May first was a Romanian holiday. The hospital would be closed, but John agreed to spend the day searching for the child's birth parents. When he returned with the news that he had found the parents and they would allow the child to be adopted, I felt blessed beyond measure. When I finally got to see the baby, Alexander, I was overcome with joy. Just like Cody, his eyes and hair were very dark and his skin olive. They were meant to be brothers; they would grow up as twins. Court officials allowed me to put in Alex's adoption papers in place of Austin's.

Meanwhile, the political climate had changed dramatically during the weeks of waiting for our court date, and things were getting heated at the American Embassy in Bucharest. The embassy officials had the authority from immigration officials to issue visas to the adopted babies. Each baby needed a visa to enter the United States. Without one, airlines would not even issue tickets for the babies. We were becoming more and more aware of the many babies that were being denied visas, making their adoptive parents unable to leave Romania with them. One by one their cases were being investigated, a process that was taking up to three months.

Some days we felt like everything would go well, but other days, especially after visiting the embassy and seeing the number of distraught parents protesting outside, we were shaken to the core. We knew that once our adoptions were final, we could very well be joining the group of about 300 families who faced living overseas for two years in order to bring their babies home.

On the day before the final court appearance, Dorise and I were very somber. We thought of our children back home. Dan had turned five while I was away and was learning to ride the bike he had gotten for his birthday. I couldn't imagine him being big enough to ride it. Carla, age eight, was crying every night because she was so worried about me. I wondered what would become of my fifth grader, Chris, who was struggling academically, and Cami, my sixth grader, who had taken over most of the household responsibilities. I gazed into their faces on the family photo I had brought with me; they now seemed to be saying, "Mommy, come home!" What would become of them if I were gone for two years?

Why did I have such promptings to come to Romania if it was going to turn out to be so disastrous for my family? Should I get on a flight home? Dorise and I talked all night and read scriptures as we tried to build up our faith and courage. I thought a lot about Moses and how we needed someone to deliver us from our bondage. I felt like the priests of Joshua who had to wade into the Jordan River before it parted for them. I realized that it was my part to stay and complete the adoptions, and then let God do his part to provide the miracle to get us home.

On Monday morning I went to the courthouse for Alex's adoption. Ours was the last case of the day. Several members of Alex's family were there, including both of his birth parents who had to appear in court for the decision. His mother was tiny. From the home study papers I knew that she lived in a two-room shack in the country with relatives and did her cooking outside over an open fire. Some Romanian newspapers reported that we were taking the babies to America to use their body parts in medical experiments, so I knew she was worried about her son. I tried to tell her in my very limited Romanian that he would have a warm home, plenty of food, and a good education.

After all the months of labor and collecting documents of every type for government and court officials, I was touched by the only two questions she asked of me. "Will you love him?" and "What will his name be?" During court she signed her name with only a thumbprint, for she could neither read nor write. As we left, she was crying. I knew she loved her son and gave him up to keep him from starving.

On Tuesday we went to court for Dorise's daughter and for Cody. I wished their parents could know how grateful we were that they were willing to give their children a better life. The hospital would have kept the babies for a time, but then they would have been sent to an orphanage. Because of all the recently enacted restrictive laws, it would have been impossible for them to be adopted. I am sure they would not have survived the coming winter of 1991-92. The orphanages were more than filled with new *abandonets*, as the Romanians called them, and food was even scarcer, since foreign aid after the revolution had slacked off.

Back at our apartment, we started the long job of cleaning up the babies. They looked sweet, but they smelled terrible. Cody was six weeks old, and Alex three weeks, but neither had ever had the birthing fluids washed from their heads. We didn't have any cribs, so we made beds for them in our suitcases. It was a huge effort to care for the babies in our primitive conditions. I got very little sleep because the next-door neighbors would pound on the walls if the babies cried at night.

Because we didn't have a washing machine or a dryer, washing our diapers and laundry was a major chore. It was always raining outside, and our apartment was so cold that things just would not dry. Cody vomited a lot, and one night he had soaked every blanket and towel I could find to put him in. Toward morning I had started to wrap him in my extra shirts.

Maria, one of our new Romanian friends, came that morning and taught me how to iron the cloth diapers and blankets so that they would dry sooner. I wanted so much to be home. Alex wasn't looking very healthy. He could only drink tiny amounts. One day his face started looking so puffy that I thought he was having an allergic reaction.

I cried and prayed each night that we could go home soon. Obtaining our documents from the court took more than a week, and getting them officially translated into English took even longer. Everyone was too busy to help us.

One night a drunken man tried to break into our apartment. Our driver's wife, Lucia, happened to be visiting us when he came pushing through the door. She was able to push him back out into the hallway. For several minutes they argued loudly, but finally she convinced him to leave. She told us he thought his drinking buddy was hiding in our apartment. I don't know what would have happened if she hadn't been there.

A few days later I was walking home from the embassy when the sidewalk near the entrance to a theater got so crowded that I couldn't move. Suddenly I felt trapped. People were pushing from behind, and I became afraid that Cody, who was strapped to my chest, would be crushed. I searched for an opening to get out into the road, which looked relatively safe. Finally, I saw an open square of mud where a tree had been planted. Just before my foot hit the mud, the Romanians near me gasped and reached out to help me. They moved aside and let me out into the road, where I was able to walk along the edge of parked cars until I was past the pressing crowd.

A few days later I was walking to the embassy on the same street when a long-haired, wild-eyed man in a military uniform pulled out a short barreled gun, placed it under the chin of a man coming down the sidewalk only three feet in front of me, and pulled the trigger. The gun did not go off. I don't know if it was a prank, or if the man was a lunatic, but my blood ran cold. I could not get myself to walk that stretch of sidewalk again.

At last in June we had the necessary papers for our visa appointments. Dorise was called up to a window for her appointment and given a visa. We were elated. She was free to return home immediately. I was then called to a different window and told that my visa request had been denied. I was instructed to wait in Bucharest until my case could be investigated.

I cannot explain how lonely, dark, and disappointed I felt after Dorise left for the United States. I was happy for her and sad for me. I was alone with two tiny, sick babies, and my money had run out. Dorise had left me what extra money she had, or I would have been destitute. We had brought with us an eight-week supply of food, and much of it was still left because we had eaten very sparingly.

On Sunday Terry called. He told me that my ward was fasting and praying for me. Many of my friends and relatives were writing letters and contacting influential people who might be able to help. Three of my congressmen were trying to intervene for me. I was surprised that they would care to help me, and I got a lump in my throat every time I thought about it. One of my Romanian friends commented, "That's what it means to be an American. Your leaders care about you." Terry told me to be sure that I had seats reserved on a flight the next Sunday because it was the last day for which my return ticket was good.

On Monday morning I went to the embassy with high hopes, but I was told that my case would take at least one month, possibly two. Even so, I swallowed my fear, and though nearly blinded by tears that I could not hold back, I made my way through Bucharest on foot and found the Tarom Airline building where I told the booking agents to save room for me and the two babies on Sunday morning's flight.

My heart was so heavy I could not bear to go back to the empty apartment. I went to the Intercontinental Hotel to look for other Americans who might be in the same situation that I now was in. Sure enough, I met several people who talked me into going back with them to the embassy, where they would check on the status of their investigations. I asked again for my status, though I had been there only two hours earlier. To my great surprise and joy, the official at the window had new information. I could see the names of my sons next to the words humanitarian paroles penciled onto a pad of paper which he held! I had not even considered this a remote possibility only days earlier because the United States Congress had placed a ban placed on humanitarian paroles for Romanian babies. A humanitarian parole would allow me to bring my babies to the United States to live. I would have to wait two years before they could apply for naturalization, but we could spend those two years of waiting at home rather than overseas.

A buzz went through the crowds of anxious parents at the embassy as the news spread. Soon Terry's telephone was ringing off the hook with calls from the spouses of others who were also stranded in Romania asking how he had done it. He referred them to our congressmen, who then called the embassy to see how I had received a parole so soon. The answer he was given did not make any sense to me. He was told that my case had already been investigated because the court had been nearby in Bucharest.

In reality, my case had not been investigated. The court for my babies had taken place not in Bucharest but in a tiny town hours away. Months later I received news of the actual investigation which took place in October. But because of the faith and prayers and fasting of my family, friends, and loved ones, God had made possible a chain of events which quickly allowed me to gain permission to bring my babies home. The intervention of God is something I cannot deny. For weeks I had watched rain-soaked parents, holding their babies outside of the embassy walls, protesting, begging for permission to bring their babies home. The slow government wheels at last began to turn on the very week of my visa request, and God blessed me to be among the first, sparing me the agony of coming to the end of my supplies of baby formula and personal food supplies, as many others had.

Lucia agreed to help me bring the babies home on the plane. The flight was supposed to leave in the early morning, but we didn't take off until noon. After a short fueling stop in Austria, we flew for the rest of the day. At about 10:00 p.m. the plane began to descend, and we expected to be in New York. To our dismay, the plane had taken us back to Bucharest, where we were unloaded and then locked into a dark terminal. Water in the rest rooms had been turned off, and there were no telephones. My babies had run out of milk, diapers, and boiled water. Without help, they could not continue the journey. Alex had gotten a horrible diaper rash from the heat of the plane. Through some iron bars, Lucia smuggled a note requesting help from her husband to a woman outside. John soon arrived and sneaked through a usually heavily guarded area to bring more milk, diapers, and water for the babies.

We had no idea why we had been sent back to Bucharest. One passenger complained to an airport worker who screamed back at him, "You fool, did you want to crash into the ocean?" Apparently our plane had not been safe.

About 2 a.m., a voice on the loudspeaker yelled at us to head out quickly to the runway. In only 15 minutes we were off again into the night. A horrible fear was in everyone's eyes. Was the plane safe? When we finally landed in New York, everybody cheered and clapped. I was ready to kiss the ground.

Our connecting flight to Salt Lake City had taken off the night before. I called my anxious husband and told him we finally made it to the United States. I was so shaken that I could hardly keep my voice under control.

We had to wait twelve hours for another flight. During the wait, it seemed as if everyone in the New York airport wanted to ask me about the two tiny babies. At one point a group of nuns gathered around. After I told them our story, the leader turned to the other nuns and announced, "Sisters, we have received our devotional for this morning. This is a remarkable story and more uplifting than the one in our manual!"

At last we were on the flight to Salt Lake and ready to land. When I heard the motor for the landing gear clunk, I knew there would be one more adventure. The landing gear had malfunctioned, and somebody had to hand-crank the wheels into place. I said one more prayer for safety. As soon as we hit the ground the pilot brought the plane almost immediately to a stop. We were thrown forward with great force, but to me it felt great. We were home.

As soon as possible we took our entire family to the temple, where we knelt at the sacred altar to have Cody and Alex sealed to our family for time and all eternity. It was the crowning moment of all that we had prayed, hoped, and cried for. We give thanks every day for each of our children and in a special way for the two boys close in age that came from Romania with love.

CONCLUSION

IN MYSTERIOUS WAYS

Not all those who traveled to Romania to adopt needy children were successful. In fact, a high percentage of couples returned to their homelands with empty arms and aching hearts. Often there were children that they had almost been able to adopt, but for one or more of a myriad of circumstances, they were forced to leave them behind. This chapter is a tribute to those who traveled to Romania in hopes of adopting a needy orphan but were met only with closed doors and empty promises.

Bryce and Karol had several friends who were going to Romania to adopt children. They had five children of their own and hadn't really thought about having more, but when they learned how desperately the children in Romania needed homes they felt they needed to help. After a powerful prompting, they prepared themselves to travel to Romania.

There never was an ideal time to adopt in Romania. With all the changing laws, each season of the adoptions had its own particular challenges. By the time Bryce and Karol were ready to travel, they heard rumors it was probably already too late. Adoptions laws would change 1 May 1991. But as May passed, adoptions were still being permitted. A new rumor circulated that adoptive parents would have to have a court date set by 1 June. Finally, when 1 June had passed and the new law still didn't go into effect, Bryce and Karol left for Romania with hopes that they could get a court date before the Romanian legislature brought the adoptions to a complete halt.

Once in Romania, they met an agent who had helped several of their friends, and he was sure he could help them adopt a baby. Before he had a chance to help them, however, they heard about an abandoned newborn baby girl in northern Romania. With very little time to work, they left immediately to see if they could arrange to adopt the newborn.

They found the baby girl in a maternity hospital. She was very tiny, and the mother had not even given her a name. They felt very fortunate, because the baby's birth mother consented to the adoption. The mother was convinced that if the baby was not adopted, it would be placed in an orphanage. Because hospital officials were not sure if new laws had taken effect, they told Bryce and Karol that they needed permission from the Adoption Commission in Bucharest to take the baby from the hospital. They tried to get an appointment with the Commission, but appointments had been completely booked for the entire year. No further appointments were being scheduled.

The lawyer representing Bryce and Karol counseled them to have the unwed birth mother remove the baby from the hospital, then adopt the baby directly from her, an option permissible by law. The baby's mother, Mirela, agreed with the plan, pleased that her daughter would be adopted.

Bryce and Karol spent every waking hour for the next two weeks gathering the documents required for the adoption and every night praying that all would go well. They named the baby Kjersty on her official birth certificate and obtained a court date.

On the decided date, Mirela reclaimed Kjersty from the hospital. Karol began to worry when Mirela would not let her hold the baby. Mirela still agreed to the adoption, but asked that she be able to keep Kjersty for one night. Karol had a feeling that Mirela would never return with the baby.

The next morning when Mirela came to see Bryce and Karol, she did not bring Kjersty. Mirela spoke at length with their interpreter and the message was clear; she wanted to keep her baby. Overnight the incredible bonding had taken place. Mirela had determined that she would do everything in her power to provide for her own flesh and blood, even in a land of poverty and despair.

It was bitter news to Bryce and Karol who had spent two weeks completing the requirements for the baby's adoption. By the time they learned that Kjersty would never be theirs, time had marched on. The new laws restricting adoptions had taken effect, and the door of possibility to any other adoption had slammed shut, coldly and firmly, in their faces.

"You should have stayed with me," their first agent scolded them as they passed through Bucharest on their way to the airport. "Now it is too late."

On 4 July, with broken hearts, they boarded the plane that carried them away from Romania. Many questions filled their minds. Why had they felt so strongly about going to Romania? What good did they accomplish? Should they have stayed with their first agent? Why did they spend so long working on Kjersty's adoption if it wasn't meant to be successful? The friends who had come with them to Romania all completed successful adoptions, and they took a little comfort in knowing that they had played an important part helping each of them.

During one of those long hours of reflection on the cheerless ride home, Bryce turned to Karol. With a new-found courage in his voice, he said something that remains with her to this day: "Who is to say that we could have given Kjersty more than her birth mother could?" It was not an easy thing to hear, but Karol knew in her heart that he was right. Little by little they began to consider that even though they were going home without Kjersty, they had accomplished something miraculous. They had convinced her frightened mother to step into the foreboding walls of that cold hospital to reclaim her daughter. She had never before even held Kjersty and had seen her only briefly during the painful birth.

With their coming, Mirela was given the opportunity to actually hold Kjersty close to her heart and look into her eyes. She began to feel for the first time the measureless love of a mother—the love that causes her to give her life, if necessary, for the sake of her baby. This young girl found that she had room in her heart to somehow find the way to provide for her daughter. Kjersty would be rocked to sleep each night, and her cries for help would be answered. The little girl would be raised as Mirela's daughter, not as an orphan.

Several months later, one of Karol's friends returned to Romania to complete the adoption of a Romanian child. The friend went to visit Mirela and found Kjersty doing very well. Bryce and Karol treasure the picture their friend took of Kjersty at home with her mother.

"Who knows," Karol writes. "Someday we may go back to Romania. The good news is that I'm now five months pregnant and everything is looking fine. I guess we had to go to Romania to convince me to have a baby of my own. I tell everyone that this is my Romanian baby through another channel because I honestly wouldn't have gotten pregnant before my Romanian experience, or if the adoption had gone through, so the Lord does work in mysterious ways."

Editor's note: If you would like to provide help for the abandoned children left in Romania, please contact your church's humanitarian department or your local civic group. Many worthwhile projects have been organized to help these children, but much remains to be done.